A Song in the Wind

A NEAR DEATH EXPERIENCE

SHARON MILLIMAN

WESTBOW
PRESS®
A DIVISION OF THOMAS NELSON
& ZONDERVAN

Scripture taken from the Holy Bible, NEW INTERNATIONAL VERSION®. Copyright © 1973, 1978, 1984, 2011 by Biblica, Inc. All rights reserved worldwide. Used by permission. NEW INTERNATIONAL VERSION® and NIV® are registered trademarks of Biblica, Inc. Use of either trademark for the offering of goods or services requires the prior written consent of Biblica US, Inc.

This book is a work of non-fiction. Unless otherwise noted, the author and the publisher make no explicit guarantees as to the accuracy of the information contained in this book and in some cases, names of people and places have been altered to protect their privacy.

Request for permission to make copies of any part of the work should be emailed to sharonmilliman@yahoo.com

WestBow Press books may be ordered through booksellers or by contacting:

WestBow Press
A Division of Thomas Nelson & Zondervan
1663 Liberty Drive
Bloomington, IN 47403
www.westbowpress.com
1 (866) 928-1240

ISBN: 978-1-5127-5590-9 (sc)
ISBN: 978-1-5127-5591-6 (hc)
ISBN: 978-1-5127-5589-3 (e)

Library of Congress Control Number: 2016914612

Print information available on the last page.

WestBow Press rev. date: 9/7/2016

ACKNOWLEDGEMENTS

I want to start by thanking God for all He has taught me through my two near death experiences and a great number of life experiences. He has shown me how great His love is. I want to thank Jesus for the great love He has shown me, especially during the times He has visited me and for all of the messages He has given me throughout my life.

Jesus, you know when I sit and when I stand. You know what is in my heart before I speak it. I am your bride and you are the Love of my soul. I carry your name. I bare your seal and wear your crown. Thank you Jesus, You are my love, my friend, my life, my light through the darkness, my Lord and Savior. I will forever praise and glorify your name.

Thank you to my wonderful husband Gary Milliman for his unending love and support. Gary, you are always there when I need you. I love you with all my heart.

Thank you to my Mom and Dad for always standing by me, for always believing in me, for always loving me, for being the two greatest influences in my life, for being two of the most precious gifts God has ever created. I love you.

Thank you, Roy L Hill, Debbie Butler, Brooke Johnson, Debi Brady, Joseph Varley,Michelle Wynn, Amy Davis, Konor Davis, Chuck Davis, Christina Ingram, Raegan, Jeffrey and Abby, Monica Wareheim, Katherine Taylor, Chris Buffa

FORWARD

By Roy L. Hill
(A SONG IN THE WIND by Sharon Milliman)

You have selected to read a book describing two near death experiences and numerous spiritual communications between realms. *A Song in the Wind* represents one of many NDE books you could have chosen. So why do I believe you should read Sharon Milliman? Despite the overlapping content with other books of this genre, *A Song in the Wind* stands as a revolutionary work. Namely, Sharon's writing focuses discussions with Jesus, the ascended Christ. I have yet to read any NDE book so devoted to direct communications with Jesus. Indeed, Jesus has much to say, not only to Sharon, but for all people of this generation. In this manner, the words of Jesus not only connect to His past ministry, but to humanity's present and future concerns.

Christians have worshiped Jesus for the last two millennia. Although many believe in the transformational power of Jesus, some limit His power to the cross and His authority to the Bible. Although crucified in body, I submit that Jesus lives in spirit right now, today! Meaning, Jesus is not preoccupied playing harps in heaven. Rather, Jesus is actively working in our lives, not just abstractly, but overtly. For with God all things are possible. To scorn modern accounts of Jesus only serves to close off possibilities by limiting the infinite power of God. Perhaps it is not surprising that Jesus rarely speaks to those who think they know everything about Jesus. Conversely, it should not be surprising that Jesus sometimes communicates directly to humble, open people, like Sharon.

Humble people exemplify the divine. They approach God like little children without precondition or doctrine. Moreover, they love without judgment or making demands on others. Pharisee types approach God as experts loaded with doctrine. They are too busy erecting monuments to ego to find time to love; they give only in expectation for return. Thus, God often uses humble, open people to communicate what is important. For instance, Jesus selected fishermen and tax collectors to serve as apostles during his earthly ministry rather than the learned or the religious elite. I believe that Jesus continues using this same wise pattern by working through humble people like Sharon.

Sharon personifies self-effacement throughout her text. In this manner, she displays a simple wisdom in her writing that transcends intellectual dogma. She also displays a pure genuineness that transcends the agenda of a self-promoting guru. Writing with humility, Sharon's paints a portrait of an ordinary person who had exceptional experiences. In this fashion, she applies everyday human experiences in sharing trials, mistakes, vulnerabilities, and simple joys. More important than these, Sharon portrays a natural love devoid of judgment or division. Be it caring for an elderly parent or helping a stranger in need, Sharon emulates Christ love through service and sacrifice. Thus, she represents the perfect kind of clay that God can mold into something beautiful. After all, what can be a better attribute than love? I cannot fathom doing anything greater while living on school earth.

Christ called Sharon to teach us all how to love through a connection with the divine. I can point to three possible means how this was accomplished. First, Jesus came to Sharon during times of trouble to provide her validation, inner peace, and future direction. In this manner, Jesus provided her the independence and strength to endure difficult trials. Second, Jesus pursued a bonded relationship with Sharon based on unconditional love. In this fashion, she learned that she was never alone and valued beyond measure. Finally, Jesus taught Sharon divine truths about trust, unity, and spiritual intimacy. Armed with divine knowledge, she now imparts great wisdom in an unpretentious manner. I believe that Sharon's style will resonate with almost every Open reader. From my perspective, her words naturally resonate as an ambassador of heaven and as an ember from the fire tended by Christ.

One does not need to be a Christian to gain from Sharon's book. Consistent with other near death experience accounts, Jesus is presented as part of heaven's unity. Sharon learned that the infinite nature of God transcends any human religion or philosophy, even while she deepened her personal relationship with Jesus. In fact, some of her experiences described do not involve Christ, but other beings tied into the unity, including God, who is the ultimate expression of Unity.

Although Sharon's story resonates with me, it may resonate less with the skeptic. After all, any good ambassador needs credibility. How do I find Sharon credible? Foremost, I find that Sharon's experiences tie into the Real. Meaning, Sharon's experiences show remarkable consistency with both the biblical Jesus and the near death experience. Most Gnostic texts do a poor job in portraying Jesus because it is difficult to fake the authority of Jesus (notable exceptions include the gospels of Thomas and Phillip). It is usually easy to spot faked near death experiences for the same reason. Sharon's presentation contains the authority of heaven, whether speaking of God, heaven, or Jesus. Although limited to high school degree, Sharon shares deep, spiritual meanings that would take volumes to explain. Although Sharon ties into what we know of the Real, there is something new and fresh to her experiences, as well. I could not help but learn from Sharon in amazement. I hope you, the reader, will also be amazed. I hope that we can all spiritually profit by this wonderful ambassador from heaven.

SONG IN THE WIND

He rides upon mystic white horses, galloping in on azure ocean waves, halting steeds' heels on fine golden sand. A breathtaking view of God's work is at hand, filling us with His love. We live through Him as we walk this land with the Spirit of God's Heavenly grace. It is with Him that our spirits are made pure and our hearts are fed. God's great love is alive and glowing within us. A song dances on the wind as He opens the yearning hearts with whispered words of ancient wisdom, love and holiness. The words that come in the wind erase all the pain, sorrow and loneliness. Each word fills our souls and our cups to overflowing. The angels spread their crystal wings and sing "Hosanna! Hosanna to the King!" Listen to their songs carried on the wind as they spread their wings announcing that King of Kings has come to free the land. As He sits upon His mighty white stallion, smiling, aglow with the Spirit as he reaches out and touches each and every hand. "Fear not! For, I am always here. I in you, you in me, the Spirit is the trinity." His face shines like the sun, His smile aglow with His holy grace. Feel God's warmth melting your heart giving life and making you new. The angel's spread their crystal wings as their song reaches a magnificent crescendo, "Hosanna! Hosanna to the King of Kings!"

INTRODUCTION

After having multiple near death experiences, I have lived a rather mystical and spiritual life due to the after affects of my near death experiences. These experiences are what are being conveyed in this book. I am not a theologian. This is not intended to be a theological book. These are the true stories of my life since my childhood. Because God comes to us all in very individual ways and He comes in ways that we each can understand, not everyone has the same kind of experiences. I hope my witness in this book will inspire the readers to reflect on the great love that God has for all of His creation.

Every life has a story. Every life has a purpose. Every person has a path they must walk. We may not always know where that path will lead, but if we are open to God, and we trust and believe in Him, wonderful things will happen. He is found in the magnificent and in the ordinary. I am writing this book not to tell you who God is to you, because no one owns that kind of knowledge, other than you. Rather, I would like to tell you what God has done for me.

CHAPTER 1

An Annointed Childhood

Compassion's Grace
By Sharon Milliman

Compassion comes all shrouded in lace. She comes loving the
whole human race.
She comes loving beyond the fear, beyond the tears of the
circumstances that life presents as tests. She comes embracing the
tests and trusting that through her faith in God, that love will
overcome all of the pain and the strife that seem to come her way.
She has learned the lesson that with forgiveness there is freedom
and the acceptance of the sorrows along with the Joys of life as well.
There is a fire that feeds her soul and she always lifts her heart in
praise to Him who gives life to all things. She knows that soon
a great wisdom will come and with it comes His Holy Grace.

Much of my life has been shaped by spiritual experiences, starting
back in early childhood. Indeed, it has been an incredible journey
for me to stand where I am today. Still, my origins are quite simple
and ordinary. I was born in Columbus, Ohio, in the 1960's, to two
loving parents and a pair of sisters. We lived in a traditional "apple
pie" American family life. Like most people, my parents worked hard
to provide a basic living; we were neither poor nor rich.

My dad was a strong, yet gentle presence in our home. He
seemed to be able to right every wrong. He also knew many of the

answers to our life questions. In my eyes, he was and is the epitome of what every man should be.

My dad worked hard and frequently traveled for business. It seemed he was often away for work and I missed him terribly as a little girl. Even though I was frightened when he was away, I believed that it was important that I be strong for my mom. I think this helped me when taking care of my mom in her later years, when she suffered from Alzheimer's disease. As described further in the book, this caretaking role connected me to many of the spiritual experiences I had later in life.

My mother was a "stay at home" mom like many women of her generation. I was happy for this arrangement because we always experienced loving security. I remember getting off the school bus, book bag and lunch box in hand, and running home as fast as my feet would carry me. There, my mom would be waiting for us at the front door. As soon as my feet hit the porch, Mom would open the door. With her beautiful face lighting up, she scooped me into her tender embrace. That was the best part of every day.

Above all else, my mother loved God and was deeply devoted to the Virgin Mary. When my mother was born, her parents dedicated her to the Blessed Mother by laying her at the foot of Mary in a special ceremony. My mother spent her entire life emulating Mary. As a child, she even wore blue and white dresses in honor of Mary. Later in life, she instilled in my sisters and I the magnitude and the holiness of being a mother. Namely, she taught us, that all life is precious and that one day we would be co-creators with God by having our own children. Through these teachings, and many others, my mother provided the ethical and spiritual bedrock that sustained me throughout my life, even to the present. Perhaps the experiences described in this book would have never occurred without embracing my mother's simple yet profound, loving faith and foundation in God.

My grandmother used to live in a sweet, little apartment down the street from a large cathedral. On a warm spring day she took us to see the cathedral. The memory still dances in my mind. Inside the cathedral was vast and beautifully bejeweled with grand art and architecture. I was breathless from the splendor and beauty of which I had never seen before. Even as a young child, I felt such a closeness to God. I saw God's beauty everywhere. As we walked down the steps of the huge church, I noticed the cherry trees that lined the steps where dropping their petals. The petals were caught up on the wings of the wind. Thousands of tiny, pink, velvet-like pearls were swirling, twirling and dancing before me. I stared in a trance; their magnificence took my breath away. I recognized something holy about the scene in front of me. Ever since that time, I had been captivated by God's amazing beauty in simple objects, the awe of God's creation, and the divine messages of synchronicities. Perhaps these early childhood experiences allowed me to be open to what God wanted to show me. I believed these messages as an adult in the same way I believed them as a child; I am still that young girl watching for God's colorful petals twirling in the air.

I continued focusing on God's natural creation as a child. Just like watching petals drop, I liked to play with sunbeams streaming into my room during the day. It is through simple nature that the Divine closely interacted with me. After I watched the sunbeams during the day, sometimes I would see angels coming out of my closet at night. More times than not, they would stand around my bed and chase away my dark childhood fears by singing sweet lullabies. One by one they would stand along the walls of my room and also by my bed. Some would be holding what looked like candles, others would be carrying boxes made of gold. They graced me with their beautiful, soft light because as a young child, I was so afraid of the dark. Only by their sweet songs, would I lose my fear and fall asleep.

My early spiritual experiences were not confined to seeing angels. In addition to my two sisters, I had two brothers who passed away shortly after they were born. One deceased brother would visit and play with me when I was about four years of age. His name was Michael.

I played with Michael every day. When I told my parents that I was playing with a boy, they said he was just an "imaginary friend." But I knew different. My brother was just as real and as solid as a person. My brother had told me to call him Jonas instead of by his real name, Michael, because he did not want to make my mother cry. She missed Michael so much and still grieved the loss.

Michael came every day and he and I really did have a lot of fun together. He was an adorable blonde-haired, blue-eyed child who loved getting into minor mischief. We used to tiptoe into the kitchen when Mom wasn't looking and help ourselves to the orange Flintstone vitamins. When Mom would make brownies for the church bake sale, we would sneak into the kitchen and pop a brownie into our mouths. Mom always seemed to catch us and she would ask me if I did it. With chocolate crumbs all over my face, I told her, "No Mommy I didn't do it, Jonas did it." When I got in trouble, my brother joined me in my punishment. For example, when my mom told me to go to my room Jonas would come too. I would tell him to sit on my bed. He joined me and he would nestle himself between my stuffed animals. All I could see was a pair of big, baby-blue eyes amongst the stuffed toys. About ten minutes later, Mom would allow me to come out of my room and we would go running to the backyard swing set. We would swing as high and as fast as we could to see who could go the highest. We used to laugh and laugh trying to touch the sky. I thought maybe I could swing high enough to give Jesus a kiss in Heaven.

My brother Michael continued to come every day for a couple of years. When we moved away he stopped visiting me. I remember one afternoon, many years after I had grown into adulthood, my mom shared that she watched me swing from her window. Amazingly, she also observed the empty swing move alongside me high into the air. Not only that, she saw Michael in the swing through her mind's eye. Thinking back, that moment would have been the perfect opportunity to tell her that my imaginary friend, Jonas, was really Michael. But I just couldn't bear the thought of causing her any pain. Although I kept silent, I suspect that my mom already knew the truth.

Michael was not the only person I saw as a young child. About the age of three or four, I remember seeing a Native American man sitting on a white horse in the wheat field behind our house. He was a distinguished looking fellow who sported long black hair and wore buckskin pants. On one occasion, I have a vague recollection of touching the horse and rubbing its ears while the man held its reins. I remember the softness of the horse's ears and the kindness of the man's smile. But still he never said a word. Like my brother, the man with the horse went away as I grew older. Although I didn't think of him often as a child, he would play a significant role later in life as an adult. Indeed, God would send them both back into my life when all seemed so hopeless and I needed an angel the most.

CHAPTER 2

THE LIGHT

The Light
By Sharon Milliman

An angel now opens a channel of pure crystalline light.
Through the Son of purest love I am set free, for He is love,
and love illuminates and lifts the shadows of the night.
His love's golden rays lift the veil so I can see
the reflections of my life's quests.
In love, I find, He is all that is,
all that was, and all that ever will be.
And now, knowing this, my soul soars high and
sings the songs of my soul's delight.
For now I have seen the Light

My First near death experience happened at the age of thirteen. Words do not fully capture the experience. I was taking swimming lessons at the YMCA in the town I grew up in. On the day of my experience, the instructor was teaching us how to dive into the ten-foot side of the pool. I did not have a good feeling about diving. I stood back and watched all the other kids dive; they all came out of the pool just fine. But when it came to my turn, I told the teacher I wasn't ready and I didn't want to do it. Despite my foreboding, the teacher threatened me by saying, "you will do this dive or I will throw you in." I walked to the side of the pool to do as I was told, but just couldn't bring myself to dive into the water. I then felt the instructor's big hands shove me into the pool. I immediately became scared, fought the water, began to sink and take a lot of water into my lungs. Finally, after what seemed like hours, I sank to the bottom of the pool. As I stopped fighting the water, my perception of events became very strange. I felt no pain or fear as I laid there on the bottom. Time seemed to stand still or became suspended. I don't know how it was possible, but I could see clearly my mother standing on the balcony at the opposite end of the pool. She was screaming while watching me drown. I could see the terror and helplessness on her face. I also saw the face of a young woman lifeguard/teacher who was on the other end of the pool with the younger children. I could hear other people screaming. The young woman screamed at my teacher to dive in and get me but he was frozen with fright. I could see the top of the water rippling and moving in slow motion. The water sparkled against the glow of a brilliant light.

I saw the bright light right above me. It was moving slowly towards me and I felt so warm and safe. Such deep love poured from this light. The light did not hurt my eyes, although it was very bright and beautiful. It seemed to move faster and become bigger the closer it came to me. I felt no pain, fear or worries. In that moment, I felt such peace that I wanted to surrender to the light. I was totally embraced by the enormous love radiating from the light. It was a love that I had never felt before and it completely enveloped every part of me. This light was about to touch me when, all of a sudden, I heard what sounded like a metal door slamming shut. Then I felt a sudden, excruciating pain in my chest. One of the other lifeguards had jumped into the water and was pulling me out of the pool. I was in agony, coughing, and throwing up all the water I had taken into my lungs. I was so frightened. I started to shake all over uncontrollably and I felt such pain in my chest and stomach. The lifeguard pulled me to the side of the pool and I felt other hands pulling me out of the water. I was still coughing up water and I felt so confused. After a few minutes of him working with me, I began to breathe normally again. I knew I was going to be just fine. Yet, I was still confused about all that I had seen and felt.

Long after I had recovered from my drowning incident, I wondered; what was that beautiful light? Namely, I wondered to the identity of this conscious light and where did it come from? At that young age, I had no answers to my questions nor did I even know how to talk about it. I never told anyone, not even my parents, about what I had experienced that day. However, I did have an "inner knowing" that whatever the Light was, it was more expansive than anything I had ever seen. Moreover, I had been changed forever because of it. It wasn't until I was older that I realized exactly what had happened that day. I still marvel at the beauty, warmth and deep love that came from that Light that I now know to be God.

CHAPTER 3

I Believe

I Believe
By Sharon Milliman

I believe that when you can take your grief and teach it to smile, you have been given strength. When you have overcome your own fear and help others to do the same, you are now brave. When you see a flower and give it your blessing, you have experienced happiness. When your own pain does not blind you to the pain of others, it is then, that you will truly know love and compassion in your own heart. When you know the limits of your own wisdom, you are truly wise, and you know you are alive when tomorrow's hope means more to you than yesterday's mistakes. Freedom is when you are in control of yourself and do not wish to control others. It is honorable when you find your honor is to honor others. Humbleness is when you don't know how humble you are, and you are thoughtful when you see me and treat me just as you would want to be treated. You are generous when you can take as sweetly as you give, and you know you are beautiful when you don't need a mirror to tell you.

My near death experience at the pool had great impact on my life. Even at a young age, I gave my life over to Jesus by making Him the Lord over my life. In this manner, I have become deeply connected with the divine. Connection with God has resulted in Jesus becoming directly involved in my life. My book describes a number of incidents where Jesus visited and talked with me. I know that this sounds incredible. But it is true. I also feel that my experiences are important because they changed my life. Perhaps my experiences may help you, the reader, in your journey.

The first time I met Jesus was at the age of fifteen. It was at that time I fully believed in Christ through first -hand experience. At this time in my adolescence, my innocence had been shattered by predatory people intruding into my life. I didn't tell anyone what had happened. I couldn't believe it myself. Not only had this situation presented itself, but I began seeing spirits one of which was my brother Michael, who I had not seen since I was a small child. I was sure other people would think I was crazy. During this time, my self-worth plummeted and I began questioning my own sanity. Already a quiet child, I became increasingly withdrawn, isolated and afraid. I even considered taking my own life.

On Good Friday, our youth choir was invited to sing at a neighboring church for the afternoon service. We arrived early to practice before the service. We gathered in the large basement to wait for our turn to sing.

A very distinct man walked into the room. When I saw this man, I knew immediately that I was in the presence of great holiness. My initial thought was that he was an apostle. But as he walked closer into view, I knew He was Jesus. He was so beautiful, I was speechless. Jesus presented as a tall man with a slim build. He had long, very dark wavy hair that fell down his back. He had an olive completion, His eyes were dark brown, and His short beard was neatly trimmed. I melted when Jesus displayed a dimple when he smiled. He was dressed just like most of us in the congregation, with jeans, a white button down shirt, and boots. It struck me as peculiar that Jesus would dress in this way. He didn't appear in white robes, as one might expect, but in a way that made me at ease. He was humble, kind, gentle and approachable - just as He had 2000 years ago.

I just sat there staring at Jesus as He walked up to me and asked "Where do I go to sit?" Meaning, He wanted to know where He should sit during the service. Jesus then sat down next to me smiling. I couldn't answer Him because my mouth was too dry and my brain couldn't form any words. I just sat dumbfounded that Jesus would choose to sit next to me.

The two women sitting in front of me also heard Jesus' question. They turned around and began telling Him where to sit in the main church. There were two younger women who also saw Him. As the two older women were conversing with Jesus, He was looking at me. He also spoke to me, smiling and in a reassuring voice He said, "What happened to you did happen. You are not crazy. I love you. I will always love you. I will never leave you. You are not alone. Don't be scared." Then Jesus stood up and as He did, He touched the elbow of the woman in front of Him. The woman had suffered from arthritis in her elbow so severe that she couldn't bend her arm. With His touch, her elbow was healed. To this day, the four women and I still talk in excited astonishment about the day we saw Jesus. Yet, none of the other choir members saw Him as He went upstairs to the main church where we were going to sing.

Jesus sat in front of a huge, beautifully ornate stain glass window that adorned the church. The choir sang the hymn, *Up to Jerusalem*. Singing in praise, I saw the sunlight stream through the window and illuminate Him. Jesus placed his hands over His face and wept. I don't remember seeing anyone else in the church that day. I only had eyes for Jesus and I sang to Him with all my heart and soul.

Why did Jesus come to me at this time in my life? I believe that Jesus wanted to validate me when I questioned my own worth, even to the point of taking my own life. Jesus did not want this to happen; He had great plans for me. After all, I had to be important if Jesus, the Son of God, took the time to tell me, in person, that He loved me. Also, I no longer felt like I was losing my mind. My experiences with Michael were real. Similarly, my sense of being victimized was credible. Before Jesus came to me that day, I had felt I had no one.

Yet, Jesus had been there for me. This was the first lesson of many that I deserved the kind of love and respect that Jesus gave me. If God respected me, then I deserved that same kind of love and respect from others as well. I thank Jesus for showing me the truth.

I knew that what I saw was real because Jesus allowed four other people to witness this wondrous event. I should add that Jesus was helpful for everyone who saw Him and even performed a miracle. Every detail was well orchestrated by divine will. I know that everything that Jesus does, He does perfectly.

People have asked me why Jesus appears to me. Ever since I was a very small child I have loved Jesus very deeply. I have always felt His presence in my life. When I was young I looked on Him, not only as the Lord over all creation, but as a big brother. Jesus and I have always had a very personal relationship; I call it a very close friendship. I have been truly blessed to have such a deep relationship with Jesus. It is a relationship that will continue to grow and deepen over time. When I falter and stumble as I walk along my path, Jesus is there to lift me up and set me back on my feet again. He is always quick to forgive; I know there is nothing that I could ever say or do, that would cause him stop loving me. Perhaps Jesus would appear more often if people sought Him as a lover of the soul rather than just a historical figure worshiped only in a building.

CHAPTER 4

GOING TO HEAVEN

In The Hills of Green and Gold
By Sharon Milliman

Come with me and stand in starlight wonder.
Feel the leaping flames of the fire aglow,
for we bring the torch of wisdom
as the seasons pass and the day turns into night.
As the ice cold, flowing waters of a spring fed river flows free from
deep within the mountains' heart and Spring breaks free after a
long winter's night.
Oh come out of your half dream and
See the hills ablaze with the moons bright gaze,
we are young and alive so come run and dance
in the hills of green and gold
For He is waiting with arms wide open.
He is the Shepherd, He is the King of Kings and He gave us the
wisdom, a world of knowledge to behold. He asks us to spread
it around to lands far and wide while He sits upon the throne
to await our return home, to the hills of green and gold,
And as you look to the sky on a cold, gray dawn, with heavy,
gray clouds hanging way down low and you feel like the world is
slipping away, just remember that He is waiting there with His
arms wide open.
And as the Spring breaks free after a long winters night see the
valley below turn green and gold

as we run like the river and fly like the eagle,
for we will all shine bright like the sun,
in this new land of the hills of green and gold.

It is rare that people have one near death experience. God felt that I needed to learn from two experiences! It was midsummer 2005; I was sitting outside on the back steps of my house talking on the phone to a dear friend of mine who lived in Oregon. It was late in the day and my husband had just arrived home from work. He had just walked passed me as I was sitting on the concrete steps. It was just beginning to rain. I heard thunder in the distance so I asked him if I would be safe talking on a cordless phone during a storm. He said I would be fine, so my friend and I continued talking as he went into the house to change clothes.

About five minutes later I heard a loud crack from a lightning bolt snaking down from an angry sky. The entire sky lit up in a brilliant silvery-white. I felt the searing pain as the lightning entered into my right arm and pass through my body. I was knocked to the ground, leaving char marks on the concrete steps where I had been seated on the steps. After passing through me, the lightning-bolt traveled under the house and blew out the transformer standing directly in front of the house. It rendered the entire neighborhood powerless for about four hours.

I was shaking all over. I was sweating and sick at my stomach. The pain in both my arm and my chest was unbearable. I could not believe what had just happened to me. Suddenly there was a force pulling me right out of my body. It felt like I was being peeled like a banana. What came next is very hard to put into words. The best I can describe it, I was floating into my house from high above. I was able to look around and could feel movement. I was very confused at this moment because everything in my house looked so strange. First, everything had a burnt yellow color to it. Even the air had this color. Next, I noticed the furniture in the house was not my furniture. For instance, the lace curtains on the windows were not my curtains! I was beginning to feel very frightened.

No one was in this house. I wondered; where was my husband? Where did my children go? Then, there was the issue of the electrical power. I knew the transformer was blown, yet I could hear what sounded like an old time radio program playing. Did I go back in time?

Suddenly I wasn't floating anymore. I was walking through the rooms looking for the radio, or whatever it was that was making the sound, but I never could find it. This must have only lasted for a couple of minutes, but time seemed to either stop or move in very slow motion.

Amazingly, I suddenly was transported into a totally new environment. I found myself enfolded within the most beautiful fluffy pink and gold clouds. They were so magnificent! I was in awe of such beauty and I felt such a deep sense of peace and complete love. The love was so big, so huge, so complete, and felt so deep. I felt like every pore of my body was open, and I was soaking all of it in. I was just basking in this deep beautiful love. I felt whole, complete and totally accepted. I had no idea what was happening. I was moving through these gorgeous clouds laterally without moving up or down. In this love, I could feel this huge conscious presence all around me. There was such a loving presence pouring love onto me and into me that I felt I was part of this love. It was a love I have no words to explain other than it was so beautiful! It brings tears to my eyes, even now.

As I was in this loving presence, two men appeared and stood one on either side of me. They were young men and looked to be in their 20's or early 30's. They were blond haired and blue eyed and wore what looked like cream colored linen clothing. There was such a brilliant glow all around them; joy seemed to pour from every cell in their bodies. I could see the detail of the tiny weave pattern of their soft, tightly woven linen clothing. Why that seemed important, I do not know, but it stood out very clearly. Perhaps the weave represented the interconnection of everything. At first I thought these men were angels but quickly realized who they were. These two men were my younger brothers who had died as babies. I just knew they were my brothers from a raw understanding in my soul. Furthermore, they looked like our father, especially when they smiled. We were so happy to see each other. It felt like a wonderful family reunion. At the time, I couldn't help but think how my dad would be so proud of them both.

CHAPTER 5

THE LIFE REVIEW

Like A Pebble
By Sharon Milliman

Like a pebble dropped into a pond our lives affect many, today
and beyond, causing ripples with what we say and do throughout
the day. One kind action, well done, can change the world for
someone or for many. Our thoughts, opinions, and attitudes are
absorbed by all, influencing moods. Never underestimate the
power of words, because what is said, is always heard, like rippling
waves, through space and time. So, keep thoughts pure, speech
positive, and actions always loving and kind. Our lives do affect
many, today and beyond, like ripples in a calm, peaceful pond.

I felt at ease in the presence of my brothers as they walked with me
from the clouds to a beautiful garden situated to the left of a huge
glorious city. There was an old stone wall at the edge of the garden
between me and the city. The wall looked like it was made of field
stone, stacked one on top of the other, with pink roses growing up
and over the wall. Although I didn't go into the city, I could see a
few distant details, including a large building with a golden dome,
other buildings and various landscapes. As I looked around the
garden, I noticed that the colors were amazingly bright and vibrant
and the air was sweet and clear. I could hear birds singing and I
heard water running, like there was a stream nearby but just out of
sight. There were immaculately-shaped trees and colorful flowers. I

felt a silken breeze and soft, cool grass touch my skin as I stood in this breathtaking place. All the while, I sensed an all-encompassing presence pouring its infinite love out onto me. I felt such joy and all I could do was stand in awe at the wonders all around me. I had an infused knowledge, or a simple 'knowing', that I had died and gone to heaven. I felt no fear, shock or dismay. I was floating in love and acceptance. It felt so good that I didn't fight it. I didn't need to. It felt right.

Loving people began to gather around me as I progressed further into the garden. Although I knew who they were, I didn't know from where I knew them. I noticed that all of these people were around the age of late 20's to mid 30's. Their skin was pink and healthy, maybe even glowing. Interestingly, they were wearing clothing from different time periods. Some of the women wore beautiful gowns while some of the men wore fancy suits. Others wore contemporary clothes, like jeans or lounge wear. It appeared to me that these people wore what they most felt comfortable in, perhaps reflecting the generation they were born to on earth. Everyone was smiling and happy. It felt very strange surrounded by so many beautiful people, yet at the same time pleasantly comfortable and familiar. It felt as if I had spent time with these people before.

Suddenly, I was shown the entirety of my life; everything I had ever said and done. It was like watching a black and white movie on a reel. It was clear that these people gathered around to offer support. There was no feeling or judgment throughout the process. It just 'was'. A huge loving presence stood behind me, pouring an overflowing love into me. It was right then that I learned God does not judge us. Rather, we judge ourselves. We stand there before God in all of His glory and perfection while we watch our lives pass in front of us. For me, all He did was love me throughout the review. Not a word was said and the review of an entire lifetime was over in what seemed like a "blink of an eye." After the review, my first thoughts were "was that it? Seriously? Oh my goodness!" I wasn't quite sure what to think about my life, but it did seem a bit incomplete. I looked at my brothers and asked "is there going to be more?" They both looked at each other and broke out in these silly grins. You may know how some brothers are, they were just smiling mischievously. I felt like they knew something I didn't. And I was kind of hoping they would let me in on it. But they didn't. I was in absolute, total and complete awe at this point at the life review and everything that had transpired since I died on my back steps.

I definitely sensed a planned arrangement to the events taking place, like the ordering of steps or phases to a story. My brothers and the others who gathered were still with me when I heard a male voice say, "What you put out into the universe will come back to you." Now, that statement really gave me pause to ponder. First I wondered where these thoughts were coming from. They didn't come from me, for I had never thought about things like this before. It seemed that I had received an infusion of divine thoughts, like some form of telepathic message from God. An explanation followed. I knew that the message meant 'good choices reap good consequences whereas bad choices reap bad consequences.' Meaning, when we put out love, love comes back. If we put out hate, hate comes back, if we put out stealing, and cheating, then these too will come back to us. Things may come back in a different way, but it will still come back eventually. In a sense, what we do to others we do to ourselves. One never knows from which direction consequences are going to come from or when. The things we think, say and do go out into the universe, gain momentum, spin, get bigger, and then come back to us like a boomerang. I don't know about you, but I'm not so sure I want to be hit in the head with a boomerang! It appeared that the opposite of love is selfishness, not hate. That hate is born out of selfishness. It also appeared that our world is in a very bad way today because of our collective selfishness. This revelation made me think that our words do have tremendous power. To be responsible in using this power, we should fill our lives with positive thoughts, prayer, beauty, and joy. Most importantly, the words that we speak are words that should build up everyone's souls, including our own.

When we are mindful of our thoughts, we can change the course of events by simply changing our thoughts. In other words, we fill our souls with the lives we choose. And what we allow into our souls comes back out into the universe.

CHAPTER 6

THE GARDEN

The Garden of Rest
By Sharon Milliman

Come . . . find rest within the beauty of the Garden. Know
that the Angels with their wings unfurled guard the golden
land, and every weary soul finds rest in God's almighty hand.
Feel the warmth of the sun, and allow the gentle breezes to
soothe the worries in your heart and calm your spirit.
Listen and breathe. Listen to the song of the ocean as it waves
in unison with the heartbeat of the Earth Mother in a constant
flow of grace. Hear the birds as they sing their songs of praise.
And as the angels and the winged ones fly with faith and
freedom, you too will spread your wings and fly, feeling
the freedom from all your worries and your burdens.
Just leave them behind as the real you, rises high
above the clouds on the wings of your eternal
spirit, your soul, which is a shining flame.
Rise up to where you belong, safely protected in the arms of
your own special angel. As you arrive you become gently aware
that you are in the Healing Garden, the temple of the Son.
Look to the green that grows all around you and at
the beauty of the flowers with their colors so rich and
vibrant. Breathe in and take in their fresh sweetness
and as you breathe, you take in the breath of God.

Feel the white wings of His peace enfold you as you feel the cool
softness of the grass beneath your feet and listen to the whisper
of the leaves on the trees as they blow gently in the breeze.
You are bathed within the colors of the rainbow to care for
each individual need. Here is a place where all is known,
where all is taken care of, by his Divine Love and Grace.
As you radiate in the glowing fire of His love, true peace
and joy replace your worries and pain for you have been
healed by the light of Christ's love, here in the garden.

As I stood there in the garden, I noticed again how beautiful and
brilliant the colors were of the flowers, trees and grass. The reds were
more red, pinks more pink, and yellows more yellow. They were
more vibrant than any colors I had ever seen on earth. The air was
sweetly fragrant, clean and clear. The sky was a gorgeous blue, like a
perfect summer day. Although it seemed like mid-day, I did not see
the sun. I did see a bright orb that reminded me of the sun, but this
beautiful white glowing light seemed to radiate from every direction.
Somehow, I knew within the deepest part of my soul that the light
was coming from the heart of God. I was absolutely awestruck by
the amazing beauty, intricacy and details of everything around me. I
could hear birds singing in the trees. I saw a stream where the water
glistened like diamonds in the sun as it flowed over the rocks. I heard
music more beautiful than anything I had ever heard before. It was
then, that I noticed, that everything in Heaven had its own pitch and
sound. The trees had a sound, whereas the leaves on the trees had
their own unique vibration. The grass also had a sound, as did the
rocks, water and so on. When you combined all of those individual
sounds, the entirety sounded like the most magnificent symphony
ever created. But this was no ordinary symphony! I knew that all
of Heaven was singing praises to God. Its beauty just poured out of
every leaf, rock, blade of grass, and every bird. In that moment I felt
a peace and joy beyond all comprehension.

There seemed to be no time in Heaven, so I have no idea how long it took for each different step of this journey. On one hand, it seemed like everything happened so fast while, on the other hand, it seemed that time stood still. I began to feel as if I was attached to a giant 'IV bottle of knowledge'. Strangely, I was being fed all this information, and I didn't even have the words to ask the proper questions. Joyfully, I received one "Aha" moment after another. I had been given the answers to all the questions of the universe. It felt like God was showing me how everything worked at the deepest level; it seemed so simple and logical. I remember at one point saying with a huge smile "Wow, is that all there is to it? That is so cool. God, you are so awesome! We humans make everything so complicated and it's really so simple."

Following the download of information, God moved His loving and accepting light in front of me. Meanwhile, I found myself examining the front of my body. I could see that I still had the same form as I did on earth. I sported the same long blond hair falling down below my shoulders. I could see my jean shorts and my feet. But I also noticed that my body felt much lighter, it felt kind of "floaty." On earth we are weighted down with gravity. In Heaven there is no gravity. Not only did I have a weightless body, but it was also illuminated. I was glowing like everything else in Heaven. I knew that my physical body was a bit of an illusion. In reality, I was made from God's loving energy. So the physical body did not really matter. Thus, I was no longer concerned about my body, how it looked, or whether I fit in or not. I did not need to judge myself before a God of total love and acceptance.

CHAPTER 7

Meeting Jesus, Spirit, and God

Free to Dance for all Eternity
By Sharon Milliman

He said, "Come, dance with me in the mist of dawn, where life
is fresh and new. Come, fill your soul with joy and laughter for
here is a place where you are free of life's pain and sorrows.
Here, is a place where tempered winds will softly blow and
your children can feel at peace. And when the flame is low,
they will dream of the comforts they had never known. Here,
you are now free to ride the winds, and see the sun, with its
golden rays. Here, you are free to see the river, as it glistens
like diamonds as it flows gracefully through the hills of green
and gold, and down to the valley, sitting way down low."
And as He holds me in His arms so gentle and so true,
there is song that can be heard as it echoes through the
emerald hills. It is a song of praise and glory. And I join
in the song, singing "Hallelujah" as I witness the miracles
before me, for at last I have been given the "eyes to see" the
majesty in every living thing and I know that I am now free
to sing and dance with Jesus, my King, for all eternity.

I was amazed to see Jesus walking out of a grove of trees into the
garden. I recognized Jesus as the Son of God by a deep soul knowing.
There was a resemblance from certain church pictures I had seen
with His dark wavy hair falling down his back, olive-colored skin

and warm dark-brown eyes. Most impactful for me was His smile that melted my heart. Jesus walked forward and began talking to me. He told me that He loved me and had walked beside me every day of my life. He told me He would never leave my side, not ever. He then told me not to be afraid. I just stared at Him speechless. He was so beautiful. To be honest, I was absolutely overwhelmed. I had always had such a deep love for Jesus ever since I was a little girl and now, I was standing with Him. I just stood there with my mouth hanging open as He professed His love for me. At that point, I no longer saw my brothers. There were still a lot of people around but my attention was solely on Jesus.

After Jesus spoke, He escorted me to the edge of the garden to a wooded glen. I watched golden sunbeams pour through the branches of the tall oak and pine trees. Under the towering branches, I noticed a log lying next to a stream with little flowers dotting the lush grass. There were even pine needles and a few pine cones scattered about. I went over to the log and sat down to listen to the water as it danced across the rocks. The air was cool and comfortable and I could hear the birds singing their sweet songs. I felt a soft silken breeze envelope me, like arms holding me, caressing me and peace filled my soul. This wasn't just any ordinary breeze; I knew that the essence of this gentle wind was the Holy Spirit.

As I sat down, I looked up and I saw a man sitting on the other end of the log next to me. I knew the man was God the Father. How I knew this I'm not sure. Maybe the knowledge came from an absolute knowing deep in the core of all that I was. In my experience, God had shoulder- length, dark, curly hair, a neatly cut beard, sparkling blue eyes, and a happy smile. He looked to be about six feet tall. He wore a white robe and sandals. God, the consciousness of all, knew exactly the perfect way to appear to me so that I felt comfortable in His infinite presence. Specifically, He appeared to me as an easily approachable man that I could trust without fear. We sat on the log together for the longest time just talking and laughing. He became silent for a moment and then turned to face me. Looking into my eyes, He asked in a quiet, gentle voice, "What would you do if it were just you and me?"

I looked at God, not having a clue what He meant, and asked, "What do you mean?"

God smiled and was patient, like a father with a young child. He asked me again, "What would you do if it were just you and me?"

I looked down at my hands in my lap, thought for a minute, and again inquired, "I don't know what you mean?" God was still smiling and very patiently said "imagine, if there were no parents, no children, no husband, and no friends, there is just you and me, no one else." Feeling somewhat intimidated and unworthy, I looked into His beautiful face, shook my head and stuttered, "No, I would drive you crazy after the first ten minutes with all my questions and chatter. Then you would not like me very much if it was just you and me." He just smiled at me with complete loving patience. He was so gentle with me that my feelings of unworthiness started to disappear. God then stood up and motioned for me to follow. We walked a short distance to the edge of the glen. Like opening a zipper in the sky, He showed me the whole universe with no one in it. There were no people, no buildings, no cars, no animals, and no trees. There was nothing but swirling, rainbow colored gases, sparkling diamond stars, and spinning planets. The entire panorama looked like a huge rainbow that stretched across the black velvet sky. It was breathtakingly beautiful, and so huge. I never realized how big the universe really was compared to our small world. Suddenly, we were back again sitting on the log by the stream. God asked me once again, "What would you do if it were just you and me?" Again, I was at a loss for the right words to properly answer His question. Meanwhile, I found myself looking at a very large oak tree in front of me. I saw the details of the trunk, such as the little life-giving veins in the tender leaves and the roots beneath the ground. What I saw was not just a tree, but the individual parts that made up the whole tree. I also saw how important all these parts were to the life of the tree. Expanding my view, I also recognized how important the tree was to the environment around the tree. Expanding my view even further, I could see how all things are connected to each other and that every part was important to the whole of creation. I studied these interconnections for a few minutes, and sensed that my noticing this was exactly what God had planned from the beginning. Then, I answered God by quoting the Koran. Now, I have no idea why I would have answered Him in this manner since I have never read the Koran in my life. But I said, "God, your hundredth name is "God is everywhere, God is nowhere and God is in me." He said, "Yes, that is right, it is, and...?"

I looked at the tree again then back at Him and said, "God, You made this tree, You are in this tree, so when I look at this tree I see You." God looked at me, smiling that beautiful smile again and He said "yes, and...?"

I started to think about my parents and I added "God, You made my parents; You are in my parents, so when I see my parents, I see You." Again He said, "Yes and...?"

"God, You made my husband, You are in my husband, so when I see my husband, I see You." He smiled and said "Yes and...?"

God was trying to get me to think further, so I began thinking that there are people in this world who are cruel, even those who have hurt me. So I said "God, there are some people who I don't really care for because they hurt others, but You made these people, You are in these people, so when I see these people, I see You."

God smiled at me again and He said "Yes, that is right. Now, I have a question for you. When you look in the mirror, what do you see?"

I looked down again at my hands and I thought for a moment. My normal response would have been something like, "I see me. I'm no one special. It's just me." Yet, I felt that that just wasn't an acceptable answer one gives to God. After all, the Creator of all things deserves a respectful and truthful answer. As I gazed into His beautiful eyes my feelings of inadequacy melted away because of the deep love I saw in their infinite depths. Then, I said "God, You made me, You are in me, so when I look in the mirror, I see You."

God replied "Yes, that is right." He seemed so happy and was smiling from ear to ear. I could feel His joy and His deep love surrounding me. I was completely immersed in His love as He looked at me. To me this was so important. I could feel the hugeness of the revelation God just taught me; I could feel it spinning in my heart and in my mind.

The lesson God taught me has been difficult for me to accept. Although, I can easily see the beauty of God in others, it is much more difficult to see God's beauty in myself. I find, even now, I have to remind myself that I am special and that I am beautiful. I have to remind myself that God doesn't make mistakes or create junk. Instead, He loves me and sees me with perfect love even though I am an imperfect being. Indeed, God's perfect love makes my soul shine so beautifully. In other words, I am perfect in my imperfections. I had struggled with low self- esteem for so many years due to other people's criticisms. Buying into their way of thinking brought me down to a place where I could not serve God properly. What I had to learn was that real beauty shines from deep within the soul. In this manner, God shines through all of our cracks. External beauty fades with time, but real beauty comes from inside and never fades. It is internal and eternal. I had to learn that my worth as a human being has to come from inside my own heart. To God I am perfect being just me. What I have to do is be happy with myself, find Joy in my life, and see His beauty deep within myself.

CHAPTER 8

TRUSTING GOD

Come Sit with Me for a while
By Sharon Milliman

Oh quiet now and rest, my beautiful little soul and be at peace,
for you are on a journey of wonder and delight. Come now and
rest with me on a beautiful star this glorious, velvet night.
Come learn, come share, come give of you and
my love and light shall pull you through.
There will be no more endless days and painful choices.
So, turn a deaf ear to the subtlety in the voices.
You need only have ears to hear the truth. The
truth is inside of you, and you know the way.
I love you my dearest little one. Just reach out and let me hold
your gentle little hand and I will help you to understand.
Oh Precious Little Soul, come sit with me for just a
while, come laugh, come sing, and share a smile.
Dear sweet child of mine, listen carefully; hear
my words, for they are set upon the wind,
Let Joy and happiness enter in, and you will hear the Angels sing.
Come out of the shadows, and be a part, this
is not the end, it's just the start.
Let my love and Joy come alive inside of your heart.
Stand up and uncover the light you try so hard to
hide, for it sparkles like diamonds in the velvet sky.
Walk straight and tall with your head held high.
For you know, you are precious in my eyes.

Let the truth conquer all. And the light of your soul
will shine bright in the Heavens for all eternity. Do
not be afraid for I will shelter you from the storm.
Dearest one, come and sit with me for a while. Rest your eyes
and feel the out pouring of my Grace. Come, sit with me for a
while. Come laugh, come sing, come share a smile. Come now
and rest with me on a beautiful star this glorious, velvet night.

While sitting with God in this magnificent garden, I watched Him pick up a stick and draw little pictures in the dirt. The pictures looked like symbols but their meaning was unknown to me. At some point during our conversation, I looked into His beautiful, crystal blue eyes and I could see His soul for just one precious moment. What I discovered there was holiness and purity, the likes of which I had never seen before. In His eyes I saw eternity revealed. In this short moment I felt as if my spirit was flying freely. Without the impurities of a disconnected life, there were no fortress walls of my own making to hold me back. In that moment we were unified; I felt completely One with Him in love beyond all human understanding. I felt an incredible freedom and peace as His love enveloped every fiber of my being. The conversation we were having stopped as we gazed into each other's eyes. We were wrapped within the silken threads of this precious moment as time stood still for what seemed like eternity. Then, suddenly, for some reason, I pulled my eyes away and looked down at my hands. He just smiled with that beautiful, fatherly smile and He too looked away, going back to doodling in the dirt with the stick that He used for drawing. We continued talking for quite a while and I felt His love surround me so completely and deeply. It was as if I was the only one He had ever created. And then I realized that no matter how huge the universe may be and how tiny I am in the grand scheme of things, I am a very important part of everything God created. Meaning, I have eternal worth because I am connected and interwoven with everything like the golden threads of a tapestry. What God taught me was every single thing He created is an extension of His love. God didn't create us to serve Him. On the contrary, He serves us so that we can learn to serve others in love with Him.

To be allowed to see God so deeply was a huge gift even though it had seemed to have lasted but a brief moment. It was in that brief moment that God had taught me how to trust Him. Although I had always loved God placing trust in Him was frightening. To me, trust meant becoming vulnerable and vulnerability usually resulted in me getting hurt. If people would hurt me, I reasoned, why wouldn't God? To be honest, I had learned the hard way through various relationships, not to trust anyone. The world had taught me over the years of my adult life that I had to build a fortress around my heart to remain safe. But in this one moment, God demonstrated that I could trust that He would never leave me. His ever- present love created a gaping hole in my defenses and those fortress walls tumbled down. I allowed God to come beyond the barriers I had placed around my heart. Trusting God allows me to love Him more fully. Loving God more fully enables me to love others with a more open heart and with unconditional love.

CHAPTER 9

THE ANGELS AT THE LAKE

Angel of Glory
By Sharon Milliman

An angel of Glory stands before me, within her delicate hands
lay a golden harp made if the sweetest dreams. And as she sings
to me her sweet lullaby, Heaven's light gently caresses my skin.
She gracefully leans in and softly whispers close to my ear, while I
close my eyes and drift to off to sleep. She says
"Look beyond earths shadows and see the majesty in every living
thing for your life is a gift and you are a child of the King. Wipe
away your tears and fear not for He guides your every step. Lift
your eyes, hold your head up high and walk with joy for He
showers you continuously with His grace. Sing out your song; let
it rise upon the wind. Rejoice and be glad as you walk the path
of holy love for what you do in love, there can be no wrong. Now
rest dear one, for when the morrow comes, the sun shall rise on
the breath of dawn. Dearest child of the King there will be many
new chances to love and sing your songs of praise to Him."

Some conversations you want to last forever. That was certainly
the case with my deep discussion with God in the beautiful garden
in Heaven. But at last God and I finished our conversation. We
proceeded to walk through the forest where we were joined by two
beautiful ornately-gowned women. They led me to a serene lake
at the end of the wooded area. I instinctively knew that the two

women were angels. To my surprise, they began showing moving pictures of future events on earth. I am honestly a bit confused by all the mixed feelings I experienced as I watched these troubling events unfold. I still felt wrapped within Gods loving embrace so I was able to endure these revelations with a certain amount of non-attachment. Perhaps my detachment stemmed from underlying shock, horror, and disbelief of what I was watching. It all seemed surreal. I was aware that the angels showed me these world events for informational purposes. I don't know why, as they didn't say as far as I can remember.

What was shown to me were horrific events that stemmed from or were a result of the 911 attacks that have led to other terrorist attacks against our country and throughout the world. Specifically, they also showed me people being killed by bombings and shootings. I witnessed our financial institutions crumbling. In the end, our money was not worth the paper it was written on. In money's place, I was shown silver and gold coins being used to make purchases. They also said that in time we would return to the barter system, as we had done long ago. They also showed me many natural disasters, such as earthquakes, volcanoes, tornadoes, and storms. Then I saw six huge waves of water covering the land. I witnessed a woman and a little boy in a car being swept off the road because of flood waters. As her car was being immersed, I saw that God had sent angels in the form of people to pull the woman and child out of the water. The boy had already died but was revived. The mother would go on to promote a series of spiritual videos. Next, they revealed how corrupt governments will become and their central role in destroying peace in our world. They were so poisoned that I saw dark clouds surrounding their capitols. In response to the corruption, I witnessed coups and rioting. I witnessed governments in different countries being over thrown and huge riots taking place in the streets. They showed me one particular riot where a man; threw something through a store front window while a nearby building burned. I also heard the sound of gunshots, and saw a man lying dead in the street. On a positive note, they revealed small pockets of light where loving people huddled in places called "safe havens." These safe havens are mostly in mountainous regions. The very last thing they showed me was a 'silver ribbon' splitting the United States apart. I was told that this 'ribbon' was a river. I felt that it was the Mississippi River, but they gave me no explanation as to the meaning of this 'ribbon' other than that the ribbon becomes larger over time. With increased flooding in the Midwest, I wonder if we are now seeing seeds of events to come.

I was surprised by the angel's revelations. I have been even more surprised and shocked when some of these events have come to pass. Sometimes I wonder what I am to do with this information other than to pray. Perhaps my experience at the lake can serve as a warning to humanity. Perhaps God was showing me that He is the Creator of the universe and all life flows from Him. He is love and all love emanates from Him. All that He created is right and good and all things are connected to God and exist in harmony with Him. When we as human beings step out of His order of doing things, when we act out of selfishness instead of love, harmony ceases to exist, and then chaos and destruction ensue throughout the world, then we are to blame, not God. God wants us to depend on Him as the ultimate source for our life and existence. Because of His great love for us, God gives us the gift of free-will. Perhaps God was showing that it's not too late to stop this horrible course of events. But it is up to us to either choose to follow God's direction or choose to follow our worldly, selfish ways.

CHAPTER 10

The Streets of Heaven

Let Peace Reign
By Sharon Milliman

Wrap us in your arms oh, sea of harmony
Sing to us your song of majesty
Share with us your gifts,
Bring us the pearls of love and peace,
Let your love flow from up above
Bring us new hope of eternity.
Give us wings so we can fly
to a new land by and by.
Angel of sweetness, Children of God,
Give praise to Him on the Most High
From the mountains we shall sing
In the valleys it will ring.
Take to flight, Oh Holy Ones
And sound the golden trumpets for we are One.
For this, is the new day that we have waited for.
Where there is no more pain, no more fear, and no more war.
It is a glorious new day, in the golden land,
Where love and peace does reign.
Look in your hearts, you will find the way,
to fill your hearts with peace today.
Let these words fill your soul
to lift your spirits and make you whole.
Take one another by the hand and

Spread the seeds of love and peace.
Help each other to understand, that
This is the new day in the golden land,
Where love and peace does reign.

What an amazing contrast between the dire visions I saw of earth in the lack and the splendor of Heaven. As briefly mentioned, I saw a magnificent city in Heaven that had been built beyond the garden wall. As I walked through the garden I saw some of the many buildings that were on the outskirts of this glorious city. Some of the buildings looked to be made out of the finest marble with tall columns gracing each building. I understood that there were buildings that served a purpose for everything one could possibly imagine. There were magnificent healing buildings with glorious pools of healing water used for soul healing for those who had had a traumatic death. Each building is attended by angels and others who are specifically trained to help souls in need. There are even special areas where small children and babies go. There, they are attended to by angels and other loved ones who are specifically trained to care for them and help them grow spiritually.

I also discovered grand halls of learning and exquisite libraries containing "books" on every possible subject. The halls of learning are not schools of science like we have here on earth but schools designed for spiritual growth. People attending the halls of learning have mentors and teachers to guide them during their spiritual quest.

There are huge, lavish banquet halls with exquisite tables heavily laden with the finest meats, cheeses, breads, and fruits. Food is not needed to sustain life in Heaven; it is manifested strictly for enjoyment. One particular banquet hall that I saw was very large and extravagantly decorated. On rich mahogany walls hung breathtaking paintings set in heavy, ornate frames. The marble floor, polished to a glass like shine, was covered with a gorgeous pink area rug. A huge crystal chandelier hung from the ceiling. A magnificent piano sat in the corner and was adorned with a crystal vase full of roses and a huge candelabra made of gold. There were many people in the room all dressed in their finest clothes. The women were dressed in beautiful gowns of every color with matching jewels that glittered in the light. The men wore dress suites or tuxes while a butler, holding a silver tray, passed around long stemmed crystal Champaign glasses. I noticed on the other side of the room, there was a table dressed in white linens and lavishly decorated with gorgeous flowers of every color in the rainbow and huge golden candelabras. The people were all smiling and talking, while some were dancing and singing to the music of the piano. It was quite festive. I don't know what the occasion was but it definitely was a celebration. I was struck by how earth-like everything appeared. Perhaps God allowed these souls to mindfully create, or manifest, such places to help them find a connection with familiar life experiences on earth. But behind every manifested object was the energy of God. In this way, it was truly the energy of love that created all things. It was love that was ultimately important, not as much the things the spiritual beings created. Beyond the city walls, I saw fertile rural areas. There are many diverse areas such as grass lands, rolling hills and prairies where our beloved animals are free to roam, including our beloved pets. They too enter heaven and are there waiting for us! As I looked around further, I noticed there were several houses or dwellings. Some were larger than others. One house was nestled among the trees on a grassy hillside with lush flower gardens sitting in behind the house. The house looked to be made of stone that changed color with the rays of the sun. Another house, made of crystal sat on a bluff overlooking what appeared to be an ocean. Each house seemed to be as unique as the individual who inhabits the house. We create what we want in Heaven, provided it does not violate the loving will of God.

In sum, I became aware that Heaven is a very busy place. There isn't time to sit around under trees eating bon bons as some may think. Rather, Heaven is an active realm with so much to do and see. Also, there is spiritual work to be done. In this manner, I noticed that people have different jobs. They were not jobs as we know them on earth but rather, jobs that help everyone further their soul's growth toward the Divine.

CHAPTER 11

COMING BACK TO MY BODY AND THE PINK BUBBLE

When The Weeping Willow Weeps
By Sharon Milliman

When the weeping willow weeps God will wipe away the
tears and lift your sorrows for if He is in every flower that
blossoms forth and in every little bird that dares
to fly, how much more does He care for you?
He is love and love cannot be measured by moments of
time but in timeless moments.
Feel the oneness with Him and allow yourself to be filled with
the glowing embers of joy and laughter.
Allow the light to shine from within you, so beautiful and
bright.
As the wind wraps around you like a silken
cloak, feel the warm and soothing
embrace, rejoice in it.
Let your spirit ride on the wind with joy and promise,
as you walk in these green, rolling hills full of sweet violets
and daffodils.
Feel the freshness of freedom as you fully awaken
to the majesty that surrounds you.
Smell the sweetness of truth and love.
Our love of God, our love for self, and our love for life, is
always, the foundation of the deepest truth.
God is love; you are love brought forth in the most
perfect way.

How should one react when paradise becomes lost? After visiting with the beautiful angels, I was sent back to my body on earth. I don't remember being given a choice. I could feel an incredible pain radiate from my right arm into my chest as my spirit entered my body. I was momentarily confused before I fully realized that I was lying on the ground in my back yard, right next to the steps where the lightning had hit me. I could see the phone knocked out of my hand lying on the opposite side of the patio. It was all burnt and black. I also saw the black char marks on the stairs where I had been sitting not long before. I was absolutely stunned by all the events that had just taken place while talking with God in Heaven. I knew my life had changed in profound ways.

It was hard for me to move because of the pain. I was shaking, sweating, and nauseous. I could barely breathe. I have no idea how long I laid there. I tried calling out, but no one came to help. It took every ounce of strength I had to move myself into the house. I found my husband and told him what had happened. I had showed him the char marks on the concrete steps and told him of the pain I was in. To my shock, he didn't care and refused to take me to the hospital. My husband dismissively replied, "I don't want to sit there waiting all evening." Consequently, I wasn't able to go to the hospital that night and remained disoriented, confused and in a great deal of pain from where the lightning struck my arm. I wasn't able to see my family doctor until a few days later. Medical tests by a cardiologist later indicated that I had suffered some minor damage to my heart as a result of the strike. I now have a condition called a Right Bundle Branch Block, which is an electrical glitch in my heart. The cardiologist told me that he had never seen anything like it before and that I was lucky to be alive. He also conducted some neurological testing to make sure everything else was working properly. Nothing else of concern was found, thank God!

After the pain in my arm subsided, I felt better than I had ever felt in all of my life. I had so much more energy than before I was hit by the lightening. One of the things I remember was I went eleven days without sleeping. Furthermore, I felt blissfully happy. That was something new for me; I felt so alive! Not only did I feel vibrant, but I could see the life force glowing from every living thing. I felt so connected with all of creation in oneness. I was totally in love with God, everything and everyone. I felt like I was floating in a pink bubble that could never burst. That's what I called it to myself because everything seemed to radiate with a pinkish glow. Amazingly, my new state gave me many heightened, extra-sensory abilities. To illustrate, I could hear the constant humming sound of electricity in the air. I could see the petals of a flower open, as if in slow motion, and observe it orientate toward the rays of the sun. I could see the blades of grass growing and spreading across the back yard. I was also able to see things several blocks away as if they were right there in front of my face. Occasionally, I was fed information from that 'IV bottle of knowledge.' These were downloads of information, similar to what I experienced in Heaven. With the information came an incredible feeling of bliss. I would only get glimpses of deep, complex information without remembering any details. Unfortunately, those bits and pieces would slip away just as quickly as they came. Yet, that 'joyful beyond words' feeling of bliss remained after each experience. I even learned over the years that I can access that knowledge and bliss when I really need it.

After my experience in Heaven, I began to perceive living beings differently. Specifically, I could see a beautiful colorful glow radiating from every plant, flower, tree, and animal. I also realized that even people have this lovely, colorful glow around them. These auras were of beautiful colors, bright pinks, and yellows, shades of gold, blues and greens. I also see bright whites or silver sparkles around people. That's an amazingly beautiful thing to see. I know that I am peering into people's soul-energy when I see their aura. This means everyone has a deeply spiritual essence guiding their lives. Furthermore, it means that every person is very close to God; for we are all walking in holiness.

There have also been times when I have seen black or gray around certain individuals. When I see this, I pray to God for them. I do this because I know that these people are having some spiritual problems and may be walking in darkness. I pray for them because I sense their pain from being lost. That's all I know how to do for them. I know God will do the rest.

During my time in the pink bubble, I spent hours sitting in silence while listening, praying, and remembering my experience in Heaven. In particular, I fondly recalled my conversations with God and Jesus. This recollection became one of my daily prayers. Other prayers were spoken in the quiet moments through an honest feeling, a kind thought, an earnest request, or a reflection. In similar fashion, God answers prayers in quiet moments. He whispers in the wind. Sometimes it is all we need just to know His presence. For example, we can see Him in the beauty of His creation. We can see Him in a sunrise and in the starry skies, or in a bird in circled flight.

As mentioned, I was downloaded amazing divine information while in the pink bubble. Some of that information was given to me in the form of poetry. In this manner, God inspired me to write about His gracious love and abundant generosity in verse. All of the poems included at the beginning of the chapters in this book were written at that time. They are from God, but they are also the muses of my heart; the visions, dreams, longings, and praise songs that come from my soul.

CHAPTER 12

A Song in the Wind

The Enchantment
By Sharon Milliman

As the wind blows the clouds across the skies, I look to the Heavens and see the brightly flickering lights which dot the velvet blackness. I see the silver moon beams dancing around me and I feel true joyfulness with an open heart. I feel the new beginnings of love and by loves transcendent glow that surrounds me, the enchantment has begun. As night turns into day, the sky becomes a radiant blue and a rainbow shines with a promise of hope renewed and the doves fill the trees two by two. There is a pink and golden glow that consumes the trees and they sparkle like diamonds in the breeze. As the doves sing their beautiful songs, I know that, like the stars in the velvet sky and the rainbow too, I am an integral part of this timeless beauty that is before me now. This knowing is within me at every moment. For we are all one with all there is, now and forever. The angelic herald is calling us to remember to live a life in the Spirit, where the lives of all who live under the stars and the moon are called to live in love as one showing forth the fruit of the Spirit which is love, peace, joy, kindness, gentleness, generosity, patience and faithfulness for all, while His love lifts us high and fills us with His Grace.

The pink bubble transformed the way I related to the world. I was less concerned about the day to day hustle and bustle of surviving and concentrated more on the little things in God's creation. In this state, I also discovered small miracles.

There were times when I could actually hear heavenly music, like a song in the wind. My heart would leap in my chest at the sound. There were days that I would spend hours just sitting in silence, listening, praying and remembering. I would find refuge in my back yard just listening to the chirping birds and feeling the wind against my skin. Similarly, I would spend hours staring at the grass and the flowers as well as watching the clouds as they floated by in a beautiful blue sky. This recollection became my daily prayer as I remembered Heaven. I never wanted to forget what I felt and heard in God's realm; I had never been bestowed a more beautiful gift. There were many times I would just start dancing because of the joy and the peace that I felt. I loved feeling all the sensations in my body. It was just like getting a sweet kiss from God every day. Before the lightning strike, I spent much of my time indoors cleaning house and mothering my two teenage children. Life was always busy; we were constantly going and doing. I never took the time to sit and be in the moment with God. I spoke *to* Him during my prayers, but I didn't speak *with* Him. Nor did I sit quiet and listen. I now recognize how much I had missed being so busy. I wanted to spend my remaining time recapturing what was really important in life. In other words, I needed to sit quietly and be still in order to hear His voice as I did when I had died. So, I made it a point each day to sit quietly and just be with God.

It was during these times, God allowed me to see that Heaven was really no further away than my own back yard. Every so often He would lift the veil to allow me another glimpse of Heaven's beauty. There were times when I would literally see the air change. I knew it was Heaven because the air was so clean, clear, and fragrant. I would see the colors of the flowers and trees become much more vibrant. Unfortunately, these experiences only lasted for one sacred moment before the world returned back to "normal." I felt such awe and joy despite the momentary nature of my experiences. There were many times I would shake myself wondering if all of this was real. Then I would hear Heavenly music come from out of nowhere. The "song in the wind" was played for me again and so I knew that it was all true.

During my near death experience, I learned that God is all about establishing a loving relationship with all of us. To my surprise, he doesn't care what religion a person selects. The question He consistently asks is "do you want a relationship with me?" For so long I had been deprived of a deep loving relationship with God. Like many people, my life had been too busy before to pay attention to Him beyond going to church and praying. But now my entire life had changed by taking the time to listen to His whispering voice stirring my soul.

There were many times I actively sought to hear God's whispering voice. Let me share a number of examples throughout the rest of this chapter.

One morning, I woke up early to watch the sun rise. Just as the sun was coming up over the horizon, I noticed all the neighborhood sounds seemed to fade away. Even the sound of the water from the patio fountain was muted. As I looked around confused, I started to hear a drum beat and chanting. Although, I didn't understand the language, the chanting sounded powerful in rhythm with the drum. I looked around but was surprised to find that there was no one out and about in the neighborhood. Because of the clear fidelity of the chanting, I knew that it wasn't a car radio or television I was hearing. The voices faded back out after a few moments as the normal neighborhood sounds faded back in. Amazingly, the chanting happened several more times during that summer. I can only guess that I was hearing the echoes of Native people who had lived in the area long ago. Just as time did not seem to exist during my near death experience, perhaps I was tuned into the past as part of a greater unity of a timeless experience here on earth.

I noticed strange events happen in the physical world during this time. For instance, I saw rainbows in the night sky. Logic told me this wasn't possible, but I cannot dispute my own eyes. I had just learned that with God all things were possible. Perhaps the rainbow symbolized that there is hope even in our darkest moments.

I also witnessed unusual behavior from animals. During an unusually warm November night, I stepped onto the patio and saw the sun shining on the two oak trees in the yard next door. This struck me as odd since it had been spitting cold, damp rain all day. The trees were beautifully lit in an unearthly golden color against a bluish purple sky. Then I noticed that a pair of doves had flown into the trees next to each other. Almost immediately another pair of doves arrived, then another, and another, until both the trees were loaded with pairs of doves. As the doves sat there in the golden trees they appeared to be a light shade of pink in the sky. Then the wind gently moved the branches. As the branches moved, the entire scene sparkled like diamonds in the light. The entire sequence of events was breathtakingly magnificent.

As this sight was unfolding the entire neighborhood sounds seemed to fade away; all I could hear was the sound of hundreds of doves' "cooing." The cooing faded after a few minutes as the neighborhood sounds faded back in. The doves began to fly away pair by pair until all were gone. Within minutes, the light faded away too and it became very dark and bitter cold outside again. There was no way it was mating season as it was much too late in the year for that to occur. Interestingly, a pair of doves is believed to be a symbol of love and fidelity. Perhaps God was showing me that He will always be faithful in His love, even during the storms of my life when I am the most worried and afraid. Doves are such beautiful, graceful birds. I love to hear their mourning songs and to listen to the whisper of their wings as they fly. Doves have always had great symbolism to me. This was another one of those "special" moments where God had moved the veil from a realm of infinite possibilities.

Jesus often used birds as an illustration of why we should not worry about what we are to eat or how we are to provide for our needs. He said, "Look at the birds of the air; they neither sow nor reap and yet our heavenly Father feeds them. Are we not more valuable than they?" Birds are such beautiful, fragile creatures, they were often held up by Jesus, as being objects of concern for the loving care of God. If God takes care of the birds, God will most certainly take care of us. When we see the birds, and how God cares for them, we know we can trust God. There is no need to worry or be afraid. God created all things. God created us in His image. We are children of God and God takes care of His own, no matter how small or fragile they might be. We can rest secure in His faithful love knowing that He provides for us, just as He provides for the birds of the air.

CHAPTER 13

SEEING SPIRITS

Spirit Breeze Song
By Sharon Milliman

We are here in the presence of the spirits of old. Where ancient
stories have been told, with these old spirits our hearts are
fed, down a sacred path our future is led. When we drift away
from what is our destiny, we are led back to where we know we
should be. Quiet your hearts and listen, so you can hear, with
a gentle breeze they will softly steer. Stories of old now come
to light. Bring out the truth, let's set it right. Ancient Spirits
guide us, so lessons will unfold. Help us to tell the stories the
way they should be told. History has rewritten the truth and
these stories once told, have come to bear fruit. Let Wisdom's
winds be your guide, knowing forever the Halls of Truth are
on our side. It matters not what has been written, nor for how
long, for real truth will come out on a Spirit Breeze Song.

After My NDE, God gifted me with the ability to discern Spirits.
This gift was very important as spirits started to approach me on a
daily basis while I was in the pink bubble. They sometimes disrupted
my day so I had to lay down some ground rules. Primarily, I would
not allow them to show me frightening things. Nor would I allow
them to wake me up at night. I continued to have visions in addition
to spirit visitation. I was grateful to God that the visions were always
very pleasing.

One day at my parent's house, I was looking out the window when a beautiful young woman walked through the yard. It struck me that she wore a long Victorian gown and a fancy hat. She also carried a parasol. Even more bizarre, the woman appeared to be transparent, although I could see the color and the details of her dress very clearly. When I saw her I became startled and yelled. The woman continued walking through the yard, across the street and into the solid bricks of the house across the street.

There were other times I would see spirits and they looked just like regular people. They appeared to me as solid. I could see their clothes, the color of their hair, and other details. I knew that they were spirits because they would appear in front of me, say a few words and then vanish. Other times, I would see them walking thru walls, cars or buildings.

I was just stunned by this altered reality beyond the perception of most people. I simply wasn't used to this. Telling my husband was a huge mistake, as it only proved to create more problems between us. My husband was not happy at all with this unusual behavior he saw in me. He felt that I was wasting too much time and not doing enough house work. Not only did he not believe me, he simply didn't care. He probably thought I was going crazy. Yet, I knew what I experienced was not hallucinations. They appeared as real as everyday reality.

It seemed that the more spiritual experiences I was encountering, the angrier and more distant my husband became. I didn't know what to do. I had no confidants close by that I could confide in. After all how could I tell my friends that I was seeing spirits almost on a daily basis? They may have had a similar reaction as my husband. So I dealt with all these spiritual visits alone. It became increasingly difficult as the activity increased. It felt like I had a blue flashing light over my head that said "If you are dead, come see me." There were times that there were so many of them that I would go to bed at night exhausted from working with them all day long. I learned not to be afraid but I also knew that I had to set down boundaries to function in my daily life.

One day I was in the living room talking to a friend on the phone when a young man appeared in front of me. He was tall with thick curly black hair, dark skin, and brown eyes. He was wearing a white tee shirt and jeans with another shirt over the tee shirt. He just stood there as I continued talking with my friend. The young man began communicating with me about how he had died and how he was connected to the person with whom I was speaking to on the phone. Specifically, he told me his name, where he had lived; he even showed me his cat. This was what I call evidential information, which I was able to pass along to my friend. Once this evidential information was given, I was then able to pass on the messages that had needed to be given. I was shocked that my friend did not dismiss my message. Rather, my friend was elated and grateful for the communication I conveyed from his nephew.

I had learned that these meetings only happen by the grace of God and according to His plan. Meaning, I cannot conjure spirits. Rather, the spirits come to me as allowed by a higher Source. God allows the spirits to approach me so that we can orchestrate a three-way meeting for a greater good. Often times, they come to me to help grieving loved ones. Other times the deceased want to resolve conflicts when they were alive. As my ability has become seen as credible by various individuals, more people have come and asked me to help them with loved ones who have passed. I do what I can to serve God's will.

CHAPTER 14

GAHANNA

Grace
By Sharon Milliman

… And now, as the sun
catches the strands of her light golden hair blowing in the
wind, something happens, like a leaf turning and turning,
caught on the breeze, for she begins to feel so deeply the
pain of the world around her and the angels in Heaven say
for her to "lean back into the arms of grace." They say to
Her, "rest, dear one, and let your tears fall like rain
that will run into the deepest blue oceans. Your heart
will heal this pain you so deeply feel and the Light
will shine upon you and you will sing again…"

God allowed me to witness the bounty of Heaven and to know the wonderful beauty of home. However, He also wanted me to know that evil does exist and that it *is* very real. God allowed evil beings to come to me as a discerning process. He also showed me how to protect myself from evil and darkness and He let me know that He was with me the whole time.

One night God allowed me to see and smell a very powerful evil being and creatures under his control. It was a night like any other night. There was nothing unusual about this particular night. My husband was working and I was alone. I was watching television and doing laundry, just doing normal everyday things when I saw them. Specifically, I remember walking into the bathroom to find little creepy creatures crawling between the wooden slats between the wall and the tub. They presented as small, grotesquely shaped creatures. They appeared very short, about knee high, and had multiple eyes; six or eight eyes scattered over their face. Oddly, it looked like their skin had melted away leaving just muscle and bone. Obviously, I had never seen anything like it before. At first, I was confused and shocked. Now, I realize that the creatures manifested themselves from dark energies, in popular horror –film form in order to show their evil and to scare me. When I finally realized what was happening, I became extremely frightened. Then I lifted the shade at the window and they were all over the house crawling up the bricks. I called the police, and they came right out and searched the house and yard but didn't find anything. So I went back to my laundry, thinking the police probably thought I was crazy. A little while later, the house began to smell a horrible stench and again I saw these little creatures. Now, they began crawling all over the outside of the house, so I called the police a second time. I called my husband at work and told him to come home. Of course, he couldn't. The police dutifully came out again and checked around to humor me. After they left, it happened yet again. This time, the house began to moan and creak loudly. I knew that I was not going insane because my dogs were barking and just going crazy. Finally, I frantically went out into the back yard when I noticed a man standing in front of me. I froze in my tracks. I couldn't figure out how he had found his way into my yard; because, we had a six foot privacy fence with a locked gate. But, there he was just standing there looking at me. Oddly, the moon light was shining down onto him like a spotlight. Something was blowing his long black hair, yet there was no wind blowing that night. He wore black pants, a black leather jacket and a white shirt. He was very handsome until he smiled. Then my blood ran cold. I was absolutely terrified. I immediately shut the door and said "in the name of Jesus, go away." Then I was immediately alone.

I will never forget that night. It turned out to be one very long and frightening night until I said "In the name of Jesus, Go away" Once I evoked the name of Christ, everything evil instantly vanished. Saying those words was automatic; it wasn't something I had to think about. Somewhere deep inside of my soul I just knew that was the right thing to say. I also knew that God had allowed that evil to appear to demonstrate that not all sprits are good. Rather, evil does exist, and that it is very real. God revealed all of this to teach me how to discern spirits. The discernment of spirits is very important, especially for people who can see beings from another realm. Certainly this lesson applied to me since I was now seeing spirits on a regular basis. I had to learn that negative spirits can be oppressive and manipulative. They can present in any form, nasty or otherwise, bringing illusion and lies whereas; good spirits bring forth light, truth, guidance, and love.

I surly know that I saw evil represented in a way that I would recognize as evil. And since that time, I have felt called more than once to pray and help others who have had issues with evil spirits. I also knew that I have to let people know the evil being I saw is a created being, just like we are created beings. Somehow I knew that he was not omnipresent, nor was he all knowing. I know there is great power in the name of Jesus. Jesus is my protection and calling on Him works every time.

Just as Heaven is real so is the Nether world. It was after my NDE, that I learned that being there, is the state of being absent from the grace of God. Not because God withdraws His grace, but by our own choice to reject His constant love and grace. When we realize that we are in separated darkness and turn to God, He will shine His light on us because He is love. Jesus came to overcome the darkness. People suffer this separation by their choices until they choose not to suffer.

Try to imagine that you are standing in God's presence and feeling His love so completely. You are seeing His beautiful face and His glorious light is shining upon you. You feel His love in every cell of your being. You feel warm, loved and accepted. Then, you look up and you see this black cloud approaching, moving closer and closer. Then the dark cloud wraps around you forming a rift between you and God. The rift is growing deeper and then forms a wide canyon. As God's light grows dimmer, you begin to feel emptier. The darkness swirls around you and you feel as if you are choking and you can no longer see God's face. The canyon is now a large gorge, an enormous deep and wide space between you and God. Now, you can no longer see anything. It is so dark and cold that you feel so alone and so hollow inside. And then you finally realize that you are all alone in the thick black void and can no longer see the Light. God is gone; He is no longer standing there with you. And all of this was by your choice. It was because of the decisions you made in your life. And then, you suddenly realize and it hits you like a ton of bricks that you walked into a desolate pit. So you sink to your knees and you cry and you scream and you wail but, no one hears you. You mourn so deeply and the pain and agony is like nothing you have ever felt before. This is being separated from God.

God is a loving God. He is not a vengeful, hateful God. He doesn't put people in this state of separation. People put themselves in this state by the choices they make in their lives.

What I learned through all of this was that God's love never ends; it is eternal. God loves everyone. Out of His great love, He has given us the gift of free-will. God is a gentleman; He honors that gift by not imposing Himself on us as we make our choices in life. Furthermore, He is a God of many chances. He is always forgiving and merciful. He never turns his back on us; but rather, He waits for us to come to Him. Even for those who no longer see the light. When we call out to Him, He will come and light up the darkness and fill us with His love. God will deliver us from our self imposed separation, and wrap us in His arms so that we will no longer feel any separation from His love.

CHAPTER 15

The Messenger

Feathery Wings
By Sharon Milliman

Feathery wings spread in graceful flight, bring to
us your joy and love with sheer delight.
Flying high on the sweet breath of God and Holy is your name
of worth. You come to us as we walk this earth, protecting
and guiding us until we reach Heaven's golden gate.
Oh sweet angel, in the pureness of His light, you lift your wings
and dance with grace, always pulling us towards Gods' Holy light.
All the while, you lift us high, to reach the
stars in the blackened velvet sky.
I see you dance and hear you sing while you play your
golden harp, a harp made of the sweetest dreams,
And smiling while you do, for you know all
things pure and good, are made of Him.
Come, Holy One, shine your light for all to see, a pure spirit
glowing white within your wings. Angel of mercy, Angel
of light, come spread your feathery wings in graceful flight
and give to us Holy peace this darkened velvet night.

I find a sense of peace and oneness with God when I am outdoors,
like when I was in the "pink bubble" after my NDE. On one
particular day, I had walked into the woods to connect and find
peace. I remember sitting on the forest floor looking up at the tall

trees into the bright blue sky with the sun streaming down through the leaves. The scene changed and I found myself sitting in a sacred familiar place. I felt as if I had come "home" and knew that God had lifted the veil of the earth to show me Heaven again. It was so peaceful with everything full and alive. I could hear Heavenly music in the air as a river and a nearby waterfall sang a pure, rich melody. As the sun peeked through the clouds the hills glowed with vibrant colors of pure gold. I heard birds sing their songs of love. Wildflowers stuck their delicate little heads through the earth while blue swallowtail butterflies flitted all around me. Thick ferns and lush moss cushioned me like a green velvet carpet. The river was a rich sapphire blue and the water was so crystal clear that I could see rainbow trout and various other fish. The trees were laden with nuts and berries and the deer were plentiful within those hills of pure gold. As I soaking up all the natural beauty, I heard the cry of the red tailed hawk as he emerged from the thick woods. As I looked up at the hawk, I saw an angel.

The angel rapidly moved forward and then stood glowing in pure white before me. I was in such awe at his magnificent beauty. A pure white light glowed from him. He said he had a message of great importance, he said "God made a promise long ago that there would always be beauty to feed your souls. You have the chance to make something special of your lives today. You are the co-creators of your own destiny. You have the power to heal your earth and stop all the wars and the pain. You have the power to stop what may be coming down the line, for you are not victims of the fates that lie ahead. You decide and you create. You do not make your lives perfect by complaining about what doesn't work or about what doesn't exist. Rather, you make your lives more perfect by valuing, learning from, and working with what does exist and what does work. You must also understand that where you are right now, this very moment is exactly where you are meant to be, by God's design. You must understand that you may not be able to change the past but you can change its effect on the present. So, you must allow God to bring peace into your world and rejoice in the mystery of creation. All the realities that you could possibly experience, or that have ever existed, exist all at once in the Divine Mind of God. Although you must have patience and allow these realities to unfold over time during your human experience, it is by your choice, your perceptions, and your intentions that lead you into one reality versus another. If you expect the best, in time you will have the best. If you expect the worst, and persist in this, you may eventually see it. All miracles and all disasters are available to be woven into the tapestry of your life. These golden threads are a reality as well. God has given you free will; you can align yourselves with His love or to feel separate from it. This is your choice. With each decision you make, you either walk with truth and with love, or you shy away from it. With each loving choice to honor your heart, and to believe in God's love and support, you walk the path of miracles. With each choice to believe, you are living your life's purpose. Conversely, with each unloving thought, you walk the path of struggle. The choice is yours and the results of such choices are the consequences you reap. You are truly blessed with the fact that God does not keep score and does not make judgments. In the end, you are the ones who do the judging. One loving choice can change the course of your entire existence, there by steering you away from all past unloving thoughts and feelings. One loving choice can change the course of your life."

I listened carefully to the angel's message and took it to heart. Of particular impact to me, I learned that one loving choice can change the course of many lives, because we are all are connected, one to the other. Although we are gifted with free-will, we are also united in the choice and breath that ultimately comes from Gods will. One loving choice can begin to change your entire life for the better. One unloving choice, such as to be unforgiving, may not mess up your entire life, but a series of unloving choices can bring fear and disillusionment. Ultimately these choices may alter the course of your life in a direction that won't serve you well. It is far better to choose a series of loving choices that creates a miraculous life.

CHAPTER 16

GRAY EAGLE

Spirit path
By Sharon Milliman

The ancestors will lead us to the sacred lands, where the
four winds blow, for there are many that surround us within
these golden hills. If you listen quietly, you will hear all that
the spirits wish for you to hear. These are the spirits of the
mountains, the valley, the rivers and streams. The deserts
and the great oceans all have stories to tell, these stories teach
us how to go with the flow on our own life's journey.
Living life from beginning to end on the Spirit Path will lead
us to the river of harmony. To live in harmony is the purpose
of every soul. Within the infinity of love in which we reside
there is a place and a purpose for all living things and harmony
flows like a river, with its own currents and its own obstacles.
Each river has its own bed that it follows. All things come as
the Creator plans. The Creator is love. Love will heal the broken
hearts you find along your path and when the Spirit gently sweeps
away the brokenness, a song can be heard that causes the heart
to sing. The Creator formed each river with love and grace.
Allow the flow of your life to engulf you. Accept the currents as
they flow before you. The sun dawns a new day as you journey
on your way, so release all that you hold bound. Be like the wind
and dance to every sacred song that the voices sing. As the long
rainbow shines, see before you, the road is straight and peaceful.
Stand and face the west wind to hear the sacred songs being sung

for a new day has come, when the Dove will fly safe with the Eagle as he spreads his swift wings. Together, they will soar gracefully through the sky, drifting high above the clouds, to a place where there is no illness and pain. It is a place, where the Blue Mountains stand tall with the rising sun and the singing waters run.

After my NDE, the Native man with the horse appeared to me again. This time he stayed with me for several years. The first thing I can say about this Native soul would be that He was a very strong spirit. He wasn't transparent like some of the other spirits I would see, but appeared very solid like you or me. Consequently, I knew that he had the power and the ability to manifest clearly in the physical plane. He appeared wearing buckskin pants and moccasins on his feet with two beautiful feathers tied in his hair. These were the same clothes he had been wearing all those years ago when he first appeared to me. But now that I was grown, I could see the magnificent beauty residing within him that I was too young to notice before. He had long dark ebony hair. His skin was the color of the earth, a reddish brown. He was tall and muscular with dark brown eyes, full lips and a strong jaw. He had a scar on his right arm that I later learned was from a knife wound from a battle won long ago. He was a warrior of very high standing; he naturally conveyed great honor and importance. When he started talking, he was speaking in a language I didn't understand. I later found out he spoke in Lakota. This proved to make communication rather difficult, even when telling me his name. He actually began showing me his name by using pictures. These were moving pictures similar to a movie.

In the beginning, he showed me that his name was Running Elk by showing me moving pictures of elk grazing on the prairie. As I watched this peaceful scene, I noticed that he was also in these moving pictures, even as he was standing beside me at the same time. He had walked slowly up to the elk. When the elk caught scent of him, they lifted their heads and began to run. He sprinted alongside, keeping up with them easily through the thick tall grass. Then, the scene stopped and he spoke to me. Still not understanding what he was saying, I finally said to him, "If you want to talk to me, you need to speak so I can understand you." Interestingly, he was able to fulfill my request, so in mid-sentence he began speaking in English. I had no idea that was all I needed to say to him. From then on, he spoke in English. He repeated his question "What did you see out there on the prairie?"

I responded "I saw Elk." He then asked, "And what were they doing?"

Again I answered, "They were running."

He nodded and smiled. Then he asked, "So what is my name?"

I answered, "Running Elk."

Running Elk responded, "Very good, you learn quickly." Then, in an instant he was gone, only to return again within the next few days, to teach me another lesson. During this second meeting, I had learned that his name had been changed to Gray Eagle. I asked him how could that be, as he had only been gone for a few days. He responded, "In Spirit World, time is different than in your world. In Spirit World you continue to grow, learn and count coup." For North Plain Native American warriors, counting coup meant to win prestige. Gray Eagle continued, "I counted coup and was given a good name." I could see that he was proud of his new name. I could feel the honor with which he carried himself and although I knew little of Native culture, I knew that counting coup was one of the highest honors given to a warrior for heroic acts of bravery. Whatever it was that he had done, it was of great importance, of that I was sure.

That was the beginning of a different, yet wonderful, relationship we shared for the next several years. I found him to be kind, wise and very patient. He had taken on the roles of protector, teacher and mentor. He taught me so many lessons that it would fill an entire book. Amazingly, I wasn't the only one who could see Gray Eagle. One evening, my granddaughter was playing upstairs while

I was downstairs in the kitchen making supper. She excitedly ran down the stairs exclaiming, "Grandma, I heard three knocks on the wall and your Indian angel wants to talk to you." Now, I had never told a living soul about Gray Eagle. Moreover, three knocks was a signal from Gray Eagle that he wanted to speak with me. When she described him accurately to the smallest detail, I became elated. This was a huge confirmation for me that what I saw was real. I thank God for allowing my granddaughter to see him.

I had an artist friend who could also see spirits. I asked Gray Eagle to go to my friend and see if my friend could draw him. I gave no details to the artist, not even a name, as I wanted the picture to be as pure as possible. When the artist was finished, the picture was amazing. The artist drew Gray Eagle perfectly; every detail was stunning. I was so excited about the picture that I wanted to show my family. When my mom saw it, she held it in her hands and exclaimed, "I remember this man. He was at my bedside in the hospital the day you were born." I easily concluded that Gray Eagle had been with me since my birth, as a spiritual guide.

As mentioned, Gray Eagle served as my teacher. He taught me that our souls do the most growing through the human experience. Interestingly, He told me on many occasions that I was "one of many nations." Meaning, I had the blood and experiences of different ethnic groups, including the Native American people. He added that I needed to be proud and honor my heritage. Curious, I had my DNA tested and learned that I am, in fact, "one of many nations." Among the many nations, I am part Native American. He told me there are many paths to get to the Creator and they are all correct. He further explained that there are many different religions and traditions that are also correct. He told me that I needed learn that these religions, these paths, are not what the Creator looks at, and evaluates. Rather, it is the person's spirit that He sees. Thus I needed to be acceptant of all faiths and learn about them without judgment. On this matter, Gray Eagle told me, "The Creator gave each culture a path toward God and they are all good." He continued to teach me the Native way. He said, "To the Indian people, the Creator is in everything. Everything is alive with the Spirit of God. The water is alive. The trees are alive. The woods are alive. The mountains are alive. The wind is alive. The Great Spirit's breath is in everything and that is why it is alive. All of nature is our church. We don't need a building in which to pray for the Creator is everywhere." He taught me that I must honor all paths, that tolerance and acceptance are very important. He said that all people are connected, we are all one nation, one family. Gray Eagle's view of inter-connection weaved throughout the fabric of time, can be illustrated in the following poem:

The Sacred Fire
By Sharon Milliman

We come before the sacred fire with humble and seeking hearts. We ask the Spirits of the Earth and the Sky to weave for us a tapestry of gold so that we may walk together, One Nation, one in spirit, all in unity. We come to this sacred place where we hear the Elders' voices as they pass through the aged pines as they sway in the breeze. The ancient ones speak with truth and wisdom that holds forever and leads us to our destiny. What can be heard are the echoes of thundering hooves on the prairie and the sound of a hundred doves in flight as the stars shine in a jeweled sky of nights gone by, a gift of the Creator to behold. Our hearts beat as one, all one nation coming to take down the imaginary walls and boundaries that separate and divide us for fear can no longer rule the land. The golden threads that run throughout the tapestry bind us all as one nation under Him who created us and the velvety darkness by the silhouette of whispering trees that speak of honor and peace and the time of One. The Elders are watching. They are waiting to show us life's mysteries. Let us walk together on this grand journey, together on common ground, to find the answers to questions many ask in words now dead and lost. It is time to bring back the sacred old ways as wild ponies gallop across the open plains, for now a new day has come and the stone walls will return as Grandfathers to the Earth once again.

One day Gray Eagle asked me to step outside and into the backyard. As I did, I looked up into the sky and saw a huge eagle flying overhead. I was mesmerized by the grace and beauty of this magnificent animal and I remembered what Gray Eagle had said about how the Creator had breathed His breath of life into this beautiful creation which made the eagle sacred. Gray Eagle began to use the eagle to teach me to look deeper into the meanings of creation. He taught, "Mankind has a way of looking at the world as if it were just black and white. Notice the eagle that flies to the sun, see how the flight feathers are black but its head and tail feathers are white. But, if you look closely there are various shades of gray in the feathers that make up the body of the eagle." Then he concluded, "Mankind needs to realize that things in this world aren't always just black and white. Man needs to see that truth is often found within the shades of gray."

Gray Eagle also taught me how to see with my spiritual eyes and not just with my physical eyes. He told me that one day he would have to leave. I was deeply saddened by this announcement and cried because my heart was broken. I pleaded with him not to leave me. Gray Eagle promised me that he never would leave me in spirit. He said, "It is easy to have faith in what you can see but the real test of faith is to believe in what you cannot see." Then he added "if you learn to see with your spiritual eyes instead of your physical eyes, you will be able to see clearer and much farther than you can possibly imagine." He taught me practical Native knowledge; for example, what it means when birds fly in certain directions, or when leaves on the trees flip over, or when moss grows on a tree in a certain direction. These are things I had never heard of before, but now I understand them by knowing how to look deeper into how creation works, how things work in unity with each other. And then, Gray Eagle did something very special. He gave me a sweet, sparkling gift.

The Morningstar
By Sharon Milliman

There's something in the air, a sweetness that I sense, warmth and beauty that permeates the air. As I look up to the sky I see them shining bright, pink and gold against the blackened velvet sky. These sacred, living, beings are alive in the night. They are beaming love and holy light, sparkling streams of light, twinkling through the clouds of cotton white. And as I look up again to see two stars joined as one, there is a sacred dance, a dance of love against a velvet sky . And as the stars whirl and twirl and spiral in their loving embrace, there is an explosion of such joy and new stars are born into the thick soft velvet night. Millions are thrown out into the Heavens, they twinkle and sparkle like diamonds leaving their mark of love, a gem filled sky. Now, as the dawn approaches, I look up again into the Heavens above and I see the gift I seek, for the two stars remain as one, pink and gold, fused together for eternity, and will forever be known as the Morningstar.

Gray Eagle appeared to me one day and took me back to Heaven. On this journey, I was not dead. I'm not exactly sure how this happened, but we did go to Heaven. I even recognized where we were at. There was a magnificent gazebo made out of mother of pearl. As he and I walked down a path towards the gazebo, I saw something sparkling beautifully in the soil. It was a beautiful diamond, the size of my hand, so I picked it up. I was so excited and said, "We need to take this home and sell it; it's probably worth a million dollars." Gray Eagle just smiled and told me that I was like that stone. He said, "You are a multi faceted diamond." Then, he wanted to show me what my soul looked like without a body. At that moment, a beautiful sparkling object appeared in his hand. It looked like one of the sparklers that children hold on the Fourth of July. He said, "Everyone has their own soul colors." My colors are rainbow colors; light pink, blue, lavender, pale yellow, mint green. Then, I asked to see what his soul looked like without a body. His revealed colors were rich, jewel tones; emerald-green, berry-red, deep- purple and pure gold.

As I was studying the difference in the colors, the two sparklers began to merge. They were spinning and swirling in a gorgeous dance. It was breathtaking to see and brought tears to my eyes. As I watched this spectacle, I noticed Jesus standing in the gazebo. I also saw that something was quietly being said between Jesus and Gray Eagle. At that point, I was suddenly returned to the flower garden sitting next to Gray Eagle. I was sitting silently with him, with wonder in my heart at all of the events that had just transpired. What an amazing gift to have actually been able to see what a human soul looks like.

CHAPTER 17

Little Dove

Little Dove (A True Story)
By Sharon Milliman

There was a little dove that came from Heaven. She was so soft, so small, and so tender. But she came with a very important message. The message she brought was one from a gracious God who breathed His love upon her then He gently kissed her and sent her to fly. She flew as fast as she could, carrying His holy words. She flew from the sun, through the clouds, to the earth below and then gently landed under a tree. As the gentle breezes blew, the little dove sat waiting for the one whom God said would come to hear her words from the Heavens above. She waited, and waited as the days turned into nights. Holding God's words and His breath within her breast, her tiny heart raced as she kept her vigil. Many days had passed and the little dove began to grow weak but she knew in her heart that God's will, would be done.

Then, one bright sunny morning, she was there, the woman with the golden hair. She had appeared just as the Lord had said she would. But now the little dove was so weak she could hardly speak. The woman with the golden hair saw the little dove lying in the grass under the tree; she walked over and gently scooped her up and nestled her softly against her heart. She took the little dove home, gave her food and water, and held her close letting the little dove feel safe and loved. The next morning, as the sun rose in a bright blue sky, the woman with the golden hair went to see the little dove and as she entered the room, she could see that the little dove was dying. She began to cry and pleaded "please don't die." Her tears poured like rain as she reached out and gently touched the little dove. She prayed that God would let her live. As she quietly sobbed, her heart breaking into a thousand pieces, the little dove slowly lifted her tiny head and in a soft little voice said, "Please don't cry. I come to you with God's holy words, and they are given just for you, they are words you seem to have forgotten.

So I must tell you before I go. God wants me to tell you, He loves you. He wants you to know and remember who you are." She said it again, "You must know and remember who you are." As the little dove said these words from the Heavenly Father, she reached her tiny head around and with her beak; she pulled a tail feather from her tail and laid it in the palm of the woman's hand. Then with her last breath, she softly laid her head down upon the woman's hand and closed her beautiful eyes. The woman, still holding the feather, could see the little dove's spirit flying free to the Heaven's and she heard the soft whisper of the dove's wings as she sat on the floor in the golden glow of the summer sun.

I was in the garden pulling some weeds in my favorite flower bed when Gray Eagle appeared. He told me about a small, injured dove lying in the alley behind our house. Concerned, I followed Gray Eagle to see this poor little bird.

When I saw her sitting there so tiny and vulnerable, I leaned down and scooper her into my hands. I nestled her against my heart, knowing deep inside that she wouldn't have long to live. I walked back home and I proceeded to look for injuries. Under her wing was a tiny scratch made by the claw of a cat. At that point I knew she would only live a couple of hours due to an enzyme under a cat's claw that is deadly for birds. So I just made the little bird comfortable by holding it to the warmth of my chest. The hour passed and the little dove didn't die, so I fed her and gave her water. She ate and drank hungrily. I was so excited; I thought maybe she would live.

Gray Eagle stood there smiling and he kept saying, "Remember who you are." The little injured dove held on for the rest of the day and through the night. It seemed like everyone from the entire neighborhood had come to see and touch the tiny dove.

When my husband came home from work and saw this, he was not happy about the crowds that had gathered. He thought it was silly to make such a fuss over a bird. I wasn't really sure how so many people found out so quickly about the little dove and I really didn't care what he thought. I felt that the more people who knew, the more could pray for her. Maybe, just maybe, she would make it. The next morning, something woke me very early and I ran into the room where the little dove lay. I could immediately see that she was dying. I reached my hand into her cage and I touched her gently. She laid her head on my hand. Then, she reached around and pulled a tail feather out of her tail and placed it into my hand. Then, she laid her head back down shutting her eyes and she died. I was so heartbroken; the tears fell like rain. After a few moments, I took the tiny body out to the rose bushes in the back yard. I wrapped her in a cloth and I gently placed her under the roses.

Gray Eagle had given me a new name that day. He had given me the name Little Dove. He had said it was a good name, that I had earned it. He had said I would be a bringer of peace and love. He said, that I understood how to be gentle and compassionate to even the smallest of God's creatures. I was very honored and thankful for the special name he gave me that day.

Gray Eagle had said several times during that day "remember who you are." This statement made me wonder, exactly what he meant. As I was considering this, Gray Eagle appeared again and he brought with him a beautiful Native woman who was dressed in a gorgeous white elk skin dress. Just like Gray Eagle, she appeared solid so I knew she was also a very strong spirit. As they approached, Gray Eagle told me she was a very holy and beloved woman among her people. I greeted the woman. She then wrapped a shawl around my shoulders and powerfully said, "Remember who you are." Then she added, "I am you and you are me. Remember who you are." Next she told me, "You have given too much of yourself away. You must stand at the four directions, call to the wind and then, call yourself back. Bring back all the pieces of yourself and become whole again." After a moment of pause, the beautiful Native woman spoke these piercing words.

"Remember who you are when the ice and snow melts away and the sun warms the earth.. And remember who you are when Spring brings a new hope and a new life and when all the first flowers begin to show their brightest colors.

Remember who you are and hold your head up high. Stand strong, walk your path in truth and light... and remember who you are when you look at the night sky with its soft and twinkling lights.

Remember who you are as you hold your babies close to your breast and as they grow they become little children. Remember who you are when you hold your children on your lap and they look deep into your eyes and your heart fills to overflowing...

Remember who you are as you hold so close to your heart the love of your family; never let them stray from the truth. Remember who you are when you look into the eyes of the most cherished friends for in love there are no bounds and we are all connected. Love is all there is...

Remember who you are when the eagle flies in circled flight and his wings touch the morning light. Remember who you are when your day has come for you have come through the storm with passion and grace. So be at Peace ... and in the end you will remember me, your soul whispers."

I still ponder the holy woman's words in my heart. She spoke great wisdom that directly applied to my life. I have always struggled to remember my magnificence, thinking that I am lesser than other people. Trying to please and become acceptable to other people, I tend to give away parts of myself. Meaning, I try to become what others want me to be like, rather than just being myself. With her words, I realized I am being disingenuous to the unique person that

God created in me. I realized that if a person can't accept me for who I am, then that relationship isn't worth pursuing. God taught me this lesson during my NDE when He asked, "Who do you see in the mirror?" Throughout the difficult challenges in my life, I somehow, had forgotten that I am a daughter of God; I no longer saw God fully in me. I had given away so much of myself just to fit in, from keeping my marriage together, to trying to make my husband happy. I tried to be so many things to so many people; I didn't even know who I was anymore. After my NDE, Gray Eagle and the beautiful holy woman reminded me, that I needed to remember that I was an heir to the Kingdom of God. I had to put the pieces back together again and fulfill my role in the Kingdom on earth. I had to call myself back because I could not continue to do God's will or be happy when there were shattered pieces of me scattered everywhere. Rather, I needed to face the four directions, call out to the wind, and bring myself back before I could move on. With a new foundation, I would move on and build a more real me.

CHAPTER 18

THE WHITE BUFFALO

In the Trail of the Wind
By Sharon Milliman

In the trail of the wind, there are many who are broken, many that feel lost, and many who await the return of truth. And so truth comes. It is carried upon the wings of an eagle as the sky fills with diamond stars, sparkling in the thick, black velvet of the night. And the drums beat loudly to the rhythm of the Earth Mother's heart as they play the sacred songs. And so we dance, we dance our prayers and we dance our sacred song. The fire rises and the smoke curls and swirls in the wind, carrying our prayers to the sky. The heat rises from deep inside as we are consumed by the flames, for our prayers can bring true all that we carry deep within. And we believe, as it was foretold long ago, that the spirits of old wander the corridors of mist in the night and with the breath of a new day, a new nation will come and the buffalo will once again roam free, just as they prayed it would. No, they did not die in vain. It is the rhythm of the dancers that brings life to the people. It is the wisdom of the old and the stories they tell that keep them alive. It is the fire of the young ones and the spirit of the people that unite us all as one family. So now we dance our prayer, we dance our sacred song, a sacred dance in the night, all nations, all creeds, dancing together in unity, no more to be lost or broken, for truth has come. The flames are rising as we dance our prayer, a sacred dance in the night.

The holy Native woman continued to be a part of my life behind the scenes for months to come. Amazingly, she celebrated me by reaching out to the Native community. A few months after her special visit, I was gifted with a white elk skin dress made by Native a woman from South Dakota. She had made the dress for me based on a vision she experienced of a holy woman. By her physical description, and the nature of the white elk skin dress, I knew that she had been visited by the same Native spirit who had visited me with Gray Eagle. Moreover, I was gifted a dance shawl from another Elder, hundreds of miles away, who had also had a similar vision on the very same day. I still keep both of these precious gifts in safe keeping.

A few months later, I was invited as a guest to A Native ceremony called The White Buffalo Messenger's Powwow. A friend of mine, who was on the board of directors for a nonprofit organization, had put on the powwow to raise funds to help support the preservation of the buffalo. Because of my previous experience with Gray Eagle and the holy woman, I was invited as her quest. While at the powwow, I had the honor and privilege of meeting and praying before the Lakota's sacred white buffalo that resided at the Woodland Zoo in Farmington, Pennsylvania. His name, Kenahkihinén (Kĕ-Nah'-Ki-Nĕn), from the Lenape language means 'Watch Over Us.' Born under extremely unusual circumstances, he is unlike any other white buffalo previously born. He is not leucistic, albino or beefalo; he is a pure white buffalo. As with other rare white buffalo born in North America, he is considered by many Native Americans to be a sacred animal. In an interesting synchronous event, a second buffalo, a black female, was born at the zoo under exactly the same unusual circumstances.1 As amazing as the powwow was for me, subsequent events were even more astounding.

About a year after the powwow, I was at home visiting with an out of town guest when I heard the words "Go to the buffalo." I told my bewildered friend that we had to drive three hours to Farmington Pennsylvania to see the White Buffalo. When we arrived, the buffalo exhibit was mostly empty. I was afraid the zoo was going to be closed because of the impending storm. Trying to beat the rain, I took off my sandals and walked the long path toward the buffalo pen. As I walked the path, I began to feel as though I had walked into another time. It was another one of those moments where God had lifted the veil and everything seemed to move in slow motion. My senses also became heightened; the colors became more vivid and the sounds were clearer. I heard the sound of a drum and chanting as I walked toward the sacred white buffalo. As I passed the cages of the other animals, they all acted in a reverent manner. I felt excitement in the air as I moved in a slow deliberate pace, while touching each passing cage. I felt like I was in a trance. Finally, I knelt in front of the buffalo pen, prepared to leave my offering. I then realized, I had nothing to give. Searching for a suitable offering, my friend provided me tobacco and I then pulled the beaded bracelet from my wrist and began to pray. As I prayed reverently, the white buffalo and the black calf walked forward and greeted me. Each bowed their heads three times. Next, they communicated affection by rubbing their bodies on a post before walking away. Just like Gray Eagle and the holy woman, they seemed to be honoring my sacred reverence for life and my identity as a daughter of God. I felt truly honored by this display. This was a truly holy moment and one I will never forget.

CHAPTER 19

OUT OF THE PINK BUBBLE

Angel in the Mist
By Sharon Milliman

An Angel in the mist, from emerald hills and golden valleys, she rises. Spreading her feathered wings, to the bluest skies, so gracefully, she flies. But, soon the skies grow angry and gray, the clouds fill with thundering storms and she can no longer fly. She is trapped in a place so delicate and ornate and this prison becomes her home. Then one day the Lord blesses her with His love and she escapes from the gilded cage, which holds her bound for so long. And in her freedom, she delights in all the beauty she sees as she sings her holy song. She is dressed all in white, so delicate and sweet, this precious dove. She rests beside a rose in the sun's golden rays and upon the wind of Heaven's love, soft petals fall from up above. When the deep, blue velvet of the night falls over sleepy garden walls and the diamond stars begin to twinkle in the sky, she leans over and kisses the night, chasing away the silver moonbeams and turning the darkness into the light. When the sun's light caresses her soft, white wings, she flies back to the emerald hills, a place where the angels sing, never again to be imprisoned within the walls of a golden cell. She flies again in the mist of the emerald hills and golden valleys, this precious dove, an angel in the mist.

So many things happened during my magnificent near death experience. But I learned very quickly that it didn't stop there. As articulated in many of the chapters in this book, everyday there was a new and different spiritual experience after I returned to earth. Although I knew that these experiences were for my spiritual growth, I needed to know why I experienced so many unusual, mystical encounters. I was particularly interested in why I encountered so many spirits. Now, I knew I wasn't crazy. But I didn't know why I experienced so many different spiritual beings whereas everyone else I knew did not. During this time, I went to see three different priests to find out why I was seeing spirits and having visions. Each one of them independently told me that it was called having the "gift of angels." Finally, there was a name for what was happening. However, none of them explained to me what the "gift of angels" meant. Although I was somewhat relieved, I was left even more confused.

Life continued in the same way for several more months. Everyday there was something more wonderful that God showed me. I was so happy after all these months living in this glorious pink bubble of love and oneness with God and creation. Unfortunately, I was not aware of something malevolent brewing under the surface. I honestly didn't realize how angry my husband had become until one day he announced that he was taking me to the hospital to be committed. He said I had completely lost my mind and my behavior warranted some kind of treatment. I was shocked by his announcement. Apparently, he had discussed this with other family members so, I didn't fight him. But didn't say a word against myself because I knew in my heart, I was not crazy. Finally, a doctor came into my room to talk with me after waiting in the hospital. He was a kind, soft spoken man who sat next to my bed and asked me, "Do you feel you need to be here?" I answered him by saying, "No, I really don't know why my husband brought me here." I had no idea what had actually been said to the doctor or nurses, so I began explaining to him what had happened with the lightning, my near death experience and all the things that occurred since. The doctor smiled at me and said he didn't feel there was anything wrong with me. He even said that if there was anything wrong, that it was other people who have the problem. He released me right then and we went home. I honestly feel that the doctor was an angel sent by God. He had a look about him that I have seen many times before; there was glow about him and a little sparkle in his eye. I have to admit I felt really betrayed and very hurt by my husbands' attitude towards me. He was becoming meaner by the minute. I was trying very hard to stay in that blissful state of the pink bubble, but it was becoming harder every day. I felt trapped like a dove in a gilded cage. I was becoming a prisoner in my home and in my life.

CHAPTER 20

I Am Sorrow

I Am Sorrow
By Sharon Milliman

Sorrow comes like a thief in the night and I cry out
for comfort. The pain is overwhelming, it shakes me
to the bone; there is no comfort, no holy light.
There is such a deep sense of loss and sadness that compares to
the fear and loneliness of a lost, abandoned child, the little girl
inside cries out for comfort, alone in the night. Compassion has
felt the struggle of bitterness and pain... So tired of climbing
the mountain alone, feeling every human emotion, yet refusing
to pass this poison on. Oh, how I pray for the light to return.
Now, I hear the echoes of my ancestors, they are calling my
name in the quiet stillness before the dawn. I hear the pounding
of the Earth Mother's heart and I hear the singing spirits' voices
on the breeze. "Don't lose heart," I hear them say as the hidden
messages are set free on the breeze. "Ride the winds of change
and you will be set free from all the chains that bind you." I listen
with a sigh for I know deep in my heart that pain and suffering
often come when we forget our oneness with the Creator and
when we forget to honor the flow of creation. So, I must reach
inside and reclaim my soul's flame and just whisper His holy
name. I must once again realize that the Spirit flows in unity
with the Source from which all things come and I will rest in
peace as I close my eyes and softly whisper His holy name.

My life felt like it was falling in on itself as my marriage came to a close. One day during this time, I was sitting outside on the back patio completely absorbed in the problems of my marriage. I was very depressed. I felt that I had failed miserably in my marriage and that I should have done something different but I didn't quite know what I could have done. Gray Eagle appeared and knelt down beside me with a semi-circle of tall angels behind me. I knew something very big was up. He gently took my hand and said, "I know how you get when your heart hurts, that is why I will tell you something." He proceeded to tell me that my marriage was over and that there was nothing that I needed to do except to "stand in peace." He said that my husband would make all the necessary moves. As it turned out Gray Eagle was absolutely right, as always. He comforted me by instructing me to "always love God and to never stray from the truth." He also told me to "speak straight like the arrow so that my words would shoot like sunlight into the hearts of others." I knew Gray Eagle was teaching me how to remain strong and how to find the courage to walk my path, even if it meant walking alone. He reminded me what God had said to me in the woods that day in Heaven. Namely, God was always with me. He had made me and was in me. God and I were united. What an encouraging reminder Gray Eagle gave me in that moment. When it was time for him to depart, he told me he had to leave for a long time and that he "could not carry me on his back forever." He said it was time for me to "spread my wings and learn to fly on my own because my wings had healed." He added that my wings were "no longer broken but, were whole and strong enough to carry me long and far." He told me that I just needed to have faith whenever I felt this was not true in moments of weakness.

Gray Eagle then elaborated as to why he had to leave. He explained that he had very important work to do for the good of mankind. He said that the Creator had asked him to do this work and so he couldn't say "no." But he said he would always be there for me if I ever needed him; he would always love me, and that I should never be afraid. He finally told me that I would see him again one day.

That was the last that I saw of him. I often wonder where he is and what he's doing. I often see an eagle flying in the sky when I think of him. I like to take that as a sign that maybe he is thinking of me too.

Gray Eagle's vision of my divorce steadily came to pass. It was well into December and we were getting ready for Christmas. My husband and I had just come home from a marriage counseling appointment that had turned out horribly. God was opening my eyes to some very important truths, including that my marriage would not last. These truths crushed me to my very core. The counseling session occurred on the day that I came out of the pink bubble. I was no longer in the familiar states of pure love and bliss. The negativity in my house was so strong, that I had shut myself down and I no longer felt anything. I wasn't happy. I wasn't sad. I wasn't angry. I wasn't anything at all. I was absolutely numb.

This numbed state lasted about six months. At first, I guessed that this inner change came from the shock of all that happened in the last several months. But I honestly didn't know, because I had no one to talk to about it. I felt so isolated and completely alone. So, I finally sought help and talked to three different priests over the following months. I also talked to a good friend who lived in Oregon. She was a very wise Native American medicine woman. I told her everything that had happened since the lightning strike. In fact, she knew of the strike because she was the one I was talking to on the phone that day when I was hit. She told me that I had undergone a Near Death Experience (NDE) and that everything I had seen and heard was typical for an NDE. She also told me that what I suffered now, was shock from the trauma of "truths" I had discovered. She also indicated that the trauma would be temporary and that the numbness would go away in time. But for now, I had to come to terms with coming out of the "pink bubble."

The changes in my life seemed to make more sense after talking with my friend. My husband still kept telling me I was crazy, but I knew that I wasn't. I had a near death experience similar to millions of other people; I was no crazier than they. I wanted so badly to go back into the pink bubble, but I didn't know how. When the numbness started to wear off, the tears started to flow and I didn't think they would ever stop. I was so unhappy. My heart was shattered; the sorrow enveloped every part of my very being. I could not understand why God would send me back to earth. Why couldn't I have stayed in Heaven? I was falling into a dark pit of despair. I especially couldn't take the cruelty of other people anymore. I had seen Heaven. I knew it was real and felt no fear in dying. So why couldn't I just leave? Although I pleaded to depart, deep down I knew that I couldn't leave. Some part of me understood that my work on earth was not done; I had been blessed with a special purpose. Although my life seemed to be falling apart, I knew that God loved me. I just needed to believe. In other words, God had given me the chance to see that I was a special person with a unique mission. I just didn't know what my mission entailed.

It was about a year later, that my husband and I split up. Our divorce was final one year after. That's when I found out that God had never left me. After the divorce, I moved out of our home and lived alone in my own apartment for two years. I was completely alone with God; there were no other distractions. It took a lot of strength and a lot of calling out to God for help to make it through all the dark nights. In fact, there were days when I could not even get out of bed. I felt that my life and everything I had known had been shattered into a million pieces. Somehow, I needed to go back in the pink bubble; I had to get back to that oneness I felt with God. As Gray Eagle has said, I needed to learn how to fly on my own. Yet, I had no idea how to do that. The pink bubble seemed so far away now. But, I did remember all the deeply spiritual experiences and other gifts from God. It felt like I still had one foot on earth and one foot still in Heaven. I just needed to reconnect to God and His love I knew to be ever present. I had to find the missing piece to reconnect to God's ever present love. Indeed, what was lost was eventually found.

CHAPTER 21

LITTLE WREN

LITTLE WREN
By Sharon Milliman

A little wren with a broken wing came to see me one day. It was a bright and beautiful, warm sunny day. As she sat there on the front porch, she said to me "I have come from the Great Woods with the dew of yesterdays' morning to bring you a gift; it is something you are losing. You will soon see this wonderful gift I have for you; but first, can you help me dear one? I am in so much pain, can't you see?" So as I went to her, I gently scooped her up as tenderly as I could and held her close to my heart. I asked the Lord and all the angels too to come and bless this tiny one, to mend her broken wing, to take her pain and allow her to fly again. I prayed and prayed. I prayed as I held her close that she would be free to fly, flying high to the great woods and to drink of the morning's rain. As I prayed these words, she laid her head upon my breast and her heartbeat slowed to the rhythm of mine.

But, after a time, the little wren lifted her head and said "Dear one, I thank you for your love and prayers. But, my pain is so severe, so I will lay my head down right here and shut my eyes; it's time for me to sleep. But, before I do, the gift I bring to you is the gift of faith. Faith, that you too can spread your broken wings. Faith that they will heal and you too will have the strength to fly free. And faith in believing that the beauty of your spirit will lift you high." She then spread her fragile, little wings one last time and laid her head down and closed her eyes. This little angel brought a message and gave a priceless gift. As I looked to the sky, I saw her spirit rise and I know that she is free, back to the Great Woods she flies.

I was sitting on my front porch trying to connect with nature by watching the sunrise. Although, I tried to spend time in God's presence, it was hard for me to fully connect with God due to the alienation I felt after my divorce. I worried that I would never connect like I did while living in the pink bubble. Worse still, Gray Eagle had left me. Imagine my doubts when I was truly alone in my physical and spiritual life. Just when I was at my lowest point, God sent me a reminder that He was still there. That morning, I audibly heard God say *"I am your shelter and your strength during the storms of your life. I am the light that guides you. I love you beyond what your eyes have seen and your ears have heard. When you can't take another step, it is then, that I will carry you. When all your hope is gone, I will give you a peace beyond your understanding and hold you close to my Heart. And when you are strong again, I will set you upon your own feet and forever walk beside you, loving you as you walk into eternity."* Just as God said these magnificent words, a little wren flew under the porch and sat there next to me. She was so tiny and precious. As she sat there next to me, I knew that she also had a divine message for me. God had sent this little bird to show me that I had lost my faith.

God gave me two incredible gifts by speaking and sending me an angel in the form of a tiny bird. Yes, I believe angels come in all shapes and sizes, including animals. The little wren was right, I had lost my faith. Faith was the missing piece in restoring my connection with God. Now that I had been shown this piece, I knew what I had to do.

After all the love I had experienced in Heaven and on earth, it was time to put that love into action in faith! In other words, I needed to step out boldly and trust that God would take care of me. So, I decided to move out of my garden apartment and into my parent's home. By moving in with my parents, I could help care for my mother, who had become ill with Alzheimer's disease. These were my first faithful steps in rising above my depression. I was able to function again and connect with God to some degree. Still I had moments of sorrow and self–doubt. Ever patient, God continued to give me messages of hope as a gift.

CHAPTER 22

THE GIFT

As I Began To Pray
By Sharon Milliman

Sitting on my window seat on a cold, stormy day; all alone
and feeling afraid, I heard these words as I began to pray.
"Believe in the miracles of every day and never lose hope, for,
hope is faith with an outstretched hand. It is there for you, a
waiting, loving hand, even in the darkest of days. So Rejoice!
Stand in this moment. This is the day you have waited for. For,
peace and love have come to the land. So reach for your dreams
and touch the stars. Listen to the voices you hear in the wind.
They speak only truth, so the truth is what you will hear." They
say, "Stand firm in your faith and truly believe that you can
weather the storm with His Holy Grace. See the angels dance
and sing. They sing Hosanna in the highest. Hosanna to the
King. You will hear it in the mountains and in the valleys it will
ring. He is the One, He is the Way. Rejoice and be glad, let no
more tears be shed for Love and Peace is born this day. Do not
be afraid. Today, you will discover the miracle that you have
been searching for. This is your Gift. It is your song. The song
in your heart will bring joy to the world. There is a message
in your song that will reach out to all. So sing it loud and sing
it strong, Hosanna in the highest. Hosanna to the King."

I had visited a priest, in order to process my anger over my divorce and the resulting pain I had suffered through those years. He asked me, "Do you consider God to be your friend?"

I assuredly answered, "Yes"

The priest advised, "Then tell Him what you are telling me. God has broad shoulders; He is big enough to handle it. If you truly consider Him your friend, then talk with Him as you would talk with a friend. Do it and just see what happens."

The priest was right. How could I have put- aside the time when God and I talked in Heaven. Furthermore, God recently spoke to me the day he sent the little wren. How easily, it seems, we slip back to periods of human self-absorption that disconnects us from God's constant presence. So, I went home and sat down on the back porch steps and began praying. I opened my heart and just poured out all my pain for God. My tears were bitter and so very deep. I told God how hurt and angry I felt. I asked him to show me that my life had meaning and that everything I had been through wasn't all in vain. I asked Him to show me that he was hearing me and that I was important to Him. I wanted Him to show me why I had to come back and that He had a plan for me. This prayer went on for a couple hours. After I had completely emptied my heart of its entire burden, I thanked Him for listening. I knew he had heard every word I had said because I prayed from the very depths of my being.

The next morning, I went outside to say my morning prayers and noticed that God had left me a gift in plain view. Right in front of me was a new bird's nest in our dogwood tree. Not only that, a mother bird was sitting on her eggs in the nest while the father bird was sitting in the next tree keeping watch over his little family. Now, this would not be a big deal to most people but it was huge to me. In my mind, bird nests symbolize new life and new beginnings. Aside from the symbolism, it takes longer than a few hours for birds to build a nest and lay eggs. But with God, all things are possible, including a miraculous nest of birds. God heard my prayer and sent me the gift that would mean the world to me. I cried with joy and

I jumped around like a little girl at Christmas time. I thanked and praised God for His precious gift in answer to my prayer. I knew He still loved me and had never stopped loving me. His love and his grace flow free and never end. Truly, I learned that, heartfelt prayers are always answered. I also learned that God knows exactly how to best answer prayers. After all, He made all of us before we entered the womb.

My life, with all the good and bad experiences in it, is a gift given to me by God. I now know that God created me and He sees me as "special." That is a gift. Every breath I take is a gracious gift from God. I want to thrive in life, not just survive. When I need help doing that, thankfully, Jesus, my ever faithful and beloved friend, will step in and do just that. He will show me that I am never alone and that my life has meaning and purpose. If I begin to have doubts, I look at the precious gift God gave me in the birds nest and I am able to face each day with hope and a prayer.

CHAPTER 23

Visit with Jesus in the flower garden

Silver Rain
By Sharon Milliman

He said, "I am sheltered" as I walk in the rain and He
wraps me so tenderly within His loving embrace.

And even though, there are silver drops falling from the
sky, the sun still shines behind the heavy laden clouds.

I can feel His love so completely. His love flows through
me and it warms me as I walk through those glittering,
falling drops that soothe the dry parched earth.

The rain comes and washes away all the dust that
accumulates over the years of walking my path. And
as I walk, the love of life brings fresh spring breezes to
scatter the gray clouds that hang low in the sky.

Now, I can see the sun breaking free, shining brightly over the
distant mountains as it dries the cool, wet, glistening silver streams
falling from the Heavens as a rainbow stretches across the sky.

I feel His caress against my cheek as I walk closer to the gift
that I have been blessed with this day and I know deep in my
heart, the depth of the love that surrounds me night and day.

I feel secure in His love, as I continue to walk ever closer to those mountains of glory that glow so bright with the sun.

And I know that one day I will rest secure wrapped tightly within His loving arms. No more to wander or walk in the silver rain.

I found it very hard to live in this world after my near death experience. I didn't know how to integrate the perfection of Heaven with my turbulent life. I found the world to be cruel and harsh and a dissolving marriage only reinforced that perception. In other words, the contrast between the meanness and selfishness in the world and the pure love of God was stark. I spent a lot of time in prayer after my divorce, trying so hard to get back in the pink bubble. The pink bubble was illusive, as I doubted myself because everyone seemed to question everything I said and did. I would often be blessed with glimpses of Heaven when I prayed to God and all the bad feelings would disappear and be replaced by moments of the blissful' joy. These were momentary reminders of God's deep love for me.

Sitting out in the back yard with the dogs, I was enjoying the soft spring breeze when I heard a noise and I looked up. It was Jesus coming to visit me. He wore that beautiful smile that I knew so well. Jesus was standing by the fence, over by the flower garden, with the sun shining down on him. Physically, He looked the same way that He always does when He appears to me. This time He was dressed in a cream colored, long flowing robe and sandals. Jesus offered me a soft pink rose from His outstretched, opened hand. Then He said these words:

"This life is a journey that all must take. Yes, you are hearing me now. You are seeing me now. Please don't question yourself so much. These messages that you are being given are true and valid. You have the answers, and you do know the truth. The answers have always been inside your heart.

Stand at your gate and take the rose, my precious Dove. It's time for you to fly. Today is a new and wondrous beginning. You were like a caterpillar all wrapped up tight inside a cocoon but you are now emerging out as a beautiful butterfly. I love you and will always love you. You will never walk alone. I walk right there beside you. So hold your head up high and always spread your joy and love.

Listen, quiet your heart and be at peace for I am always with you. If you don't hear me talking, it's because you are not listening. You have the courage and the strength to do all that your heart desires and all that My Father has called you to do. It has been shouted from the highest mountains and heard in the lowest valleys. Its whisper has been heard throughout all human experience. So you must trust that it is true.

Trust and believe, with all of your being that LOVE is the answer. It is Agape Love, meaning pure unconditional love that is the answer. Believe in and expect miracles, for they will happen. When you quiet your mind and spirit, answers will come.

My Father knows you. He knows that when you go into nature you will find rest. Nature is where you will become one with all that is, all that was, and all that will ever be. Know that in this place, you will find your greatest peace and joy. You will never walk alone. Not ever, all those who went before you, are all around you, loving you and supporting you in your walk on this earthly plane.

Open your heart and don't be afraid. Just cast all your fears aside and accept your new life. Just be at peace. Remember this; I am in you and all around you. Turn wood and you will find me. Lift a stone, I am there. Like the sun warms your skin, I will touch you, and as the rain washes you, I will also. Without you I am nothing. With you, I am eternity."

I love Jesus and because of my personal relationship with Him, Jesus is not just some religious figure as He knows me so intimately. Because He knows me perfectly like the wood and the stone, He knows my every need. He knew exactly what I needed to hear at that exact moment. When Jesus handed me the pink rose, I noticed that it was made of a beautiful silk material that would never wither. I actually felt like a princess for the first time in my life. Jesus had lifted my self-esteem so high with just that one simple act. Jesus had given me a tangible gift that represented His love, gentleness and grace. When I look at my rose today, I am reminded to open my heart, to love others, and to love myself the way God loves me.

When I was in the pink bubble, I was cocooned, sheltered, and held within Gods own hand. At that time, we were One. It was my mountain top moment. But there is a season for everything. By affirming that everything that was happening was real, Jesus was telling me that I was not the same person that I was before my NDE. When I came out of the bubble, that season was over. It was time to come down off the mountain and reenter the world and become a butterfly. Jesus was telling me it was time to grow spiritually and witness Agape love to the world.

It takes fortitude to witness love to the world. Jesus was encouraging me to let go of the self doubt, fear and low self esteem that had plagued me most of my adult life. I was no longer bound as a prisoner in my own back yard. In other words, He was asking me to step beyond my gate, to trust and believe that I was far more than I recognized in myself. I was no longer the cocooned caterpillar readying in the pink bubble, but a splendid butterfly spreading her wings to fly into the dizzying heights. Flight was possible because He was always with me in my heart, pumping strength into my soul through His tender love. Jesus stated that, as a butterfly, I would do all that the Father wanted of me. What a comforting message, that I would be of good service to my Creator.

Finally, I learned that I would co-create my unique life, because I never walked alone. Jesus promised He would always be with me. Because Jesus was always by my side, I did not need to go to other people to learn the truth. Rather, I only needed to go to the One truth that was written on my heart. Although my path would be long and hard, I know this was a journey I had to take, as we all do.

Yet, there was no reason to be afraid when all the dirt of the world gets washed away by Jesus, just as if it were washed away by the rain. Besides, I was told to expect miracles! With Jesus, I know that I can find the miracle of peace whenever turmoil comes my way.

CHAPTER 24

PRAYER

As I Await the Dawn
By Sharon Milliman

As I sit in the shadows, awaiting the dawn, silver
moon beams cast their glow upon my brow,
And I am bathed within the morning song. I close
my eyes and smile at the sweet sound as
I hear the calling of the mourning doves
as they sing their sweetest lullabies.
It is love that they declare in the songs that they sing. As the dawn
approaches, my soul soars high to meet the angel of light, where
love awaits with unfurled wings ready to take flight. The angel
then opens a channel of pure crystalline light. It is through the
Son of purest love, that I am set free. For, He is love, and it is His
love that illuminates and lifts the shadows of the darkened velvet
sky. His loves' golden rays lift the veil so I can see the reflections of
my life's quests. And, in love I find, He is all that is, all that was,
and all that ever will be. Now, knowing this, all of my fear and
doubt have been lifted and cast away with the night. \And my soul
soars even higher upon the gentle wings of a dove, as the sun glows
brighter chasing away the shadows of the darkened velvet night.

Having a high degree of empathy for other people and their suffering,
I asked God a series of questions; "why do bad things happen to
good people; do you listen to my prayers? Why do so many people

suffer? Why do some people's prayers get answered and some seem to be ignored?" That evening during my prayers I was looking through my bible and I came across a hand written poem. It was written on a worn and tattered piece of paper. As I opened the paper and began reading the words, I knew the words were from God and He was answering my prayers.

I Asked God

I asked God to take away my pain God said "No, It is not for me to take away, but for you to give it up."

I asked God to make my handicapped child whole. God said," No, her spirit was whole, her body was only temporary."

I asked God to give me happiness. God said "No, I give you Blessings. Happiness is up to you."

I asked God to spare me pain. God said "No, Suffering draws you apart from worldly cares and brings you closer to me."

I asked God to help me love others, as much as He loves me. God said "Ahhhh, finally you have the idea."

Author unknown

This poem strongly resonated with my interactions with God. As for my question about returned prayers, I knew my answer through my own life experiences. God never ignores my prayers; He responds to my pleas and tears. I found that I can discover answered prayers by searching for unexpected responses, not just through my own wishes. For example, if I pray for someone's healing and they die, then God answered my prayer in the most perfect way. He took my loved one home to be with Him. He truly healed them completely. In situations like these, I understand that God sees the bigger picture, whereas I cannot see very far ahead.

The universe does not revolve around any one human being. Most often we do not know what is best for ourselves. God taught me that sometimes He says "yes," sometimes "no," sometimes "wait," and many times "it is up to you to decide." Whatever decisions we make, we are here on earth to learn from both our successes and our mistakes. More specifically, we are here for a short time to learn how to love. In this manner, we become God's hands, His feet and His voice in this world. God will not end all the suffering on earth. Rather, it is up to us, as the body of God, to help end the suffering by loving and helping others. The best way for evil to prosper is for good people to do nothing. There are far too many good people in the world for us to allow the level of suffering in the world to continue.

Through my prayer, I became aware that God gifted me with the inner resources and the talents to help the suffering. Even if it is only one person that I am able to help, then I have done an important part in answering God's will for my earthly mission.

God does love us. He never leaves us but He wants us to take responsibility for our mission to learn how to love and to act in love. God has not failed the ones that are suffering, people have failed them. If I sit by and do nothing, then I have failed them too. Mother Teresa once wrote, 2 *"I used to pray that God would feed the hungry, or do this or that, but now I pray that he will guide me to do whatever I am supposed to do, what I can do. I used to pray for answers, but now I am praying for strength. I used to believe that prayer changes things, but now I know prayer changes us and we change things."*

Suffering is an inevitable part of life. But it does have a purpose. We can try to run from it or we can allow it to transform us in unimaginable ways. We can allow it to make us angry and bitter at God, or we can allow it to teach us how to love more fully.

I don't always get what I want in this life, but I know with all my soul that God hears every heartfelt prayer and He provides everything that I need. He has shown me over and over how much

He loves me. I know with all my heart that God sent me back from Heaven to show that same love toward others by how I live. I have learned that the deepest level of prayer involves praising God in spite of my pain, thanking God during my trials, trusting God when I am tempted to quit and loving God when He seems far away. At my lowest, God is my hope. At my darkest, God is my light. At my weakest, God is my strength. At my saddest, God is my comforter. When I cannot speak, He knows my heart. When I cry, my tears become my prayer. Sometimes simple words are all I can say. For instance, I might pray, "More of you, Lord, and less of me."

One of the most profound realizations from my NDE is that God is Love and everything that comes from God is love. Because of His love for us, everything He does for us is gratuitous Love.

Grace is everything, God created me to know me, to love me, to serve me in this life so that I could be with Him forever in the next life. He accomplishes this by the gratuitous giving me His Holy Spirit who teaches me who I am and empowers me to live the life God designed for me.

God desired His creation to be an object of his love. Therefore, He created us so He could love and serve us. God gives all by pouring grace continuously into us. Our response to God's love is to serve the needs of creation and to help each other understand that we are the object of His love. We are not here to serve God, He serves us. But at the same time, we are here to love and serve each other.

CHAPTER 25

Marriage and another Visit with Jesus

Meadows of Emerald and Lace
(A True Experience in a Field of Flowers)
By Sharon Milliman

As she walks through meadows of emerald and lace, the sun shines upon her radiant face. Her eyes are crystal blue; the color of the sky, her skin is soft and fair as the petals of a rose. And, as the sun shines upon her, her hair glistens like threads of spun gold. She is clothed in purest white as she waits for her groom. The King of Kings will arrive very soon, for He comes to claim this fair maiden, His precious bride. As she walks through meadows of emerald and lace, she is full of God's love and showered by His grace. Now with the sounds of trumpets, the skies open wide and her bridegroom appears. Truly alive with the deep love that she feels, it overwhelms her and brings her to tears. He descends from His throne and she runs to Him. As He gathers her gently within His embrace, He says to her "well done my beloved, it's time to come home." He then places a crown of diamonds and gold upon her brow and gently takes her hand as she climbs each every stair, for she knows not what awaits her there; for eyes have not seen, nor ears have heard the glories of the Lord.

After my marriage fell apart I felt disposable and replaceable. I was different inside and out and my ex-husband didn't like these differences. When someone has such a profound spiritual event like an NDE, they fundamentally change. However, when I returned from Heaven, my understanding and commitment to marriage only deepened.

I came back with a new awareness of the kind of love that could hold up under the weight of a real relationship. Meaning, when I came back, I had a deeper understanding of what a true marriage commitment meant. Since that time I have remarried and I am currently in a wonderful, loving marriage. What I learned, is that marriage signifies a sacred union between the two people and God. It means two become one with God and in God. During my NDE, the love I experienced was a love beyond words because it was transforming and all encompassing. It is the kind of love where one desires to lay down their life for another. That is the kind of love that I have found with my new husband.

I purchased a regular colored dress for our wedding because, I had been married before. As the day of our wedding drew near, a video was sent to me anonymously on my computer. The video was a song called '*The Wedding Day*' by Casting Crowns. The song touched my soul because it reminded me of when Jesus had come to me just a few years before.

Around the time I was preparing for my marriage, I had an amazing but puzzling interaction with Jesus. It had been a long tiring day, taking care of my mother who was afflicted with Alzheimer's disease, so I went out into the back yard to take a walk. My parents' yard reminds me of a botanical garden with many varieties of flowers and blooming trees. It's quite lovely and it's a wonderful place to find rest and peace. But on this day, I was very agitated and distraught, even though I was surrounded by nature. Overwhelmed by my mother's condition, I began pacing up and down the walkway. It was during this pivotal moment that Jesus appeared.

Jesus was standing amongst the bright yellow day- lilies beside my parent's patio. He greeted me with a beautiful smile, as always. What was unusual, Jesus was dressed in a fine white suit with His dark hair pulled back behind His neck. He looked as if He was going somewhere formal. Jesus asked me, "I love you, will you be my bride?"

I was quite stunned by this question. Wide-eyed and face flushed, I answered, "I can't marry you! I have to take care of my parents. Besides, I am old enough to be your mother. And why would someone who looks like you want to be with someone who looks like me?"

Jesus just smiled and very patiently explained, "You don't understand. I love you and my love for you has nothing to do with what you look like." I continued pacing back and forth not quite understanding the intimacy and quality of the conversation taking place. Then Jesus invited me again, "Will you be my bride?"

Thinking that every bride must leave her parents home, I knew I just had too many responsibilities taking care of my sick mother, I just couldn't leave. I asked, "Where would we go?"

Jesus answered, "My kingdom is not of this world."

I told Jesus that I could not go with Him because I had too many responsibilities caring for my parents.

Jesus smiled so tenderly at me and said "I love you and I will wait for you." I was still pacing the walkway and, as I turned around, saw that Jesus was gone.

I had to smile. Jesus always speaks tenderly of His deep love and leads me into a place of quiet, peaceful stillness. Just the touch of His hand heals my life's wounds. The look in His eyes speaks of the love in His heart. I feel a union of hearts- a spiritual intimacy that leaves nothing unsaid.

After Jesus had left I realized that He wasn't inviting me into a physical marriage. Rather, Jesus was inviting me into a deeper, more spiritual relationship. I have come to understand that Jesus is the bridegroom and that all of us, men and women alike, are His bride. As the Bridegroom, Jesus is dressed in justice and virtue. His vows blessed in His mercy, love and faithfulness. Jesus wants a more personal relationship with all of us, one as emotionally intimate as that of a bride and bridegroom. I have come to realize that it is through my relationship with Him that I gain the strength to carry out the difficult responsibilities that I have in my life. I think that is why He appeared to me when I became overwhelmed in taking care of my mother. He wanted to support me through this difficult period with His ever deep-well of love.

Remembering my visit with Jesus and having seen the video, I changed my mind about wearing an ordinary dress for my wedding. I knew it was right for me to wear white. I knew that my new marriage would be patterned after my relationship with Jesus. Putting my love for Jesus first in my life allows me to love my husband even deeper.

What became very clear to me is that my marriage to my new husband is about loving him unconditionally and unselfishly. When I think about the conversation I had with God in Heaven, I think about the words that I said to Him, "God you made my husband, you are in my husband, so when I see my husband, I see You." When I remember these words, I see my husband with different eyes, and my love for him grows deeper. Because of the love I have for God and the love I have experienced in God, everyday there is a renewal of the marriage vows we made together.

CHAPTER 26

How Much Do You Love

The Celebration of life
By Sharon Milliman

I raise my eyes to the Heaven's, giving
praise for the breath I breathe.

I can feel Him all around me. I savor the feel of His touch as He
wraps me in His perfect love; for there is no other and we are one.

He touches me in the morning light as the
dew rests upon the sweet Earth.

It sparkles as the mist is blown away with Heavens' gentle breeze.

He raises me up to the highest mountains and
allows me to see the golden meadows below.

He sings to me His songs of love and joy fills my soul.

He calls me to dance with Him in the fields of pink and
gold as peace fills my soul. I feel refreshed and renewed.

This is a celebration of life; for He is in all the
beauty I see and in every sound I hear. For,
It is Gods' voice that I hear in the wind and
in the fluttering of angels' wings.

Having an NDE gave me a new perspective on life. Whatever we do in our lives, however big or small the act may be, pleases God if it is done out of love. In the twilight of life, there is only one question that will be asked, "How much did you love?" Truly, in the end, love is all there is. There are people who will accomplish grandness in life, either through wealth, winning over others, or by fame. Although they are esteemed in the world's eyes, these accomplishments mean nothing to God if their works are not done for and in love. Conversely, it means everything if what is done, is done in love.

God does not measure accomplishment as people do on earth. Most people live simple, ordinary lives, accomplishing simple, ordinary things. These accomplishments may seem insignificant to the ambitious. Many love in simple ways like fixing dinner for the family, doing laundry, picking up trash alongside the road, caring for an injured bird, planting flowers in the garden, giving money to someone who can't afford medicine, caring for children, talking to a friend who is sad, caring for aged parents, or sitting with someone who is sick or dying. Although, these are not world changing events, they are monumental acts done out of love. I have learned that to God, small acts are just as important as big acts. These small acts of love are immensely important to God because, they can change the world one little bit at a time. In fact, loving one another is pretty much the purpose of our lives here on earth; to love one another, to lay down our lives for each other, to rid ourselves of our selfish ego and live in love and service for each other.

I was mopping the kitchen floor during a particularly difficult day taking care of my mother, when I had a visitor. I made a promise to God, when I was a little girl, that I would take care of my parents when they were in their older years and I intended to keep that serious promise. But there were some days where I felt as if I had failed her in some way. Some days the burden could be very overwhelming especially when I had to watch my own mother disappearing right before my own eyes and knowing that there was nothing I could do to help her. I felt so helpless. At that particular moment, I was not really thinking of anything, just mopping away and trying to decompress when all of a sudden I heard a familiar male voice. It was a smooth, calming voice that made my heart sing and my soul soar. Jesus had returned to visit me.

I turned around to find Jesus standing in the kitchen leaning against the counter with his arms crossed over his chest and his feet crossed at the ankles. As always, He was smiling at me. Standing still with the mop in my hand, I could feel His love so deeply. I didn't have to say a word because Jesus already knew my heart. He knew what I was feeling. Jesus looked into my eyes as tears streamed down my face and He said:

"Oh my precious Dove, you cry because you think I cast you away when you were with me in Heaven and that is so far from the truth, I hold you so dear. It simply wasn't your time. I have a job for you to do.

My beautiful little one, you know that I love you. You know that I am with you. I always am. You are here because your life has meaning. You have to step aside and take the "you" out of the equation. You are doing just fine, in what you are doing. Because what you do, you do out of love. Don't be so hard on yourself. Just let me do the work. I will handle it. I am capable. You just be. Just be present and be at peace. You just love, the way you always do.

All that has happened to you in your life, has happened to prepare you for this moment in order to make you strong enough for this very important job I have asked you to do for me. I am with you to give you my strength. I love you. Lean on me when you are weak and scared. Do not be afraid. Just love, that's all. Just Love. It's that simple. That is the purpose of your life, my beautiful Dove. When you feel torn and weary, give it to me; remember, I am strongest when you are at your weakest. Don't worry, I won't leave you stranded. I am right here with you always. I will love you until beyond the end of time"

Jesus visits me at the times when I need Him the most. It was very comforting to hear Jesus affirm my care for my mother. I understood that I didn't need to be afraid of the future, even living with someone with Alzheimer's disease, because Jesus was taking the burden on himself. He is always there to encourage and give me strength to carry on in this life. He raised me up in strength when I became overwhelmed in my weakness and self-doubt. He brought me peace and order to my chaotic world by revealing that the answers to some very hard questions in my life were amazingly simple. What a Relief! I didn't need to figure out complex solutions to life's messy problems. All I had to do was love and let Jesus do the rest. No matter what hurdles come along in my life, everything will be just fine because Jesus will never leave me stranded. Life is always changing but Jesus is the one constant in my life. He is the same yesterday, today, and forever.

CHAPTER 27

A CHILDS PROMISE

The Butterfly
By Sharon Milliman

The butterfly emerges from its silken shell - Reborn, it arises, no
longer bound to earth. Free at last, the butterfly glides to heights
unknown before.
So, do our loved ones find a beautiful release, as earthbound
no more, they leave our sight and joyfully rise to a garden
of matchless beauty, a place of light and peace

When I was a young girl, I made a promise to God that I would
care for my parents when they were in their older years and I have
always tried to honor that promise. I never really knew what that
promise would entail and in truth, it doesn't really matter. I would
do anything for them. I adore my parents, and caring for them
is an honor and a privilege. Caring for them brings more joy and
purpose to my life than I could have ever imagined. My parents took
responsibility of me during my childhood and I want to lovingly give
back to them with gratitude. I am able to do this by helping and
taking care of them as they grow old. I won't hesitate to repay them
the kindness and loyalty they gave to me. My parents were my first
ally in this world. I cherish them, thank them and love them every
day for the life they have given me.

As I wrote this book, my mother had become afflicted with
Alzheimer's disease. She had the disease for about eight years. It

was an extremely difficult journey but also a very joyous one - one I would not have traded for the world.

As every day passed, I could see my mom disappearing right before my eyes. It was frightening. When I began caring for my mom, I didn't know anything about Alzheimer's disease. So, I did as much research as I could. I found simple card games and puzzles that would interest her. I found out that routine and structure helped to keep her engaged and sociable, almost up to the very end of her life. Every day we had our routines. We would get washed and dressed, eat breakfast, and then we would take a walk at the park. If it was a nice day, we would go out to lunch. We would come home and do crafts, play cards, or do puzzles. Then, it was time for a nap. When she woke up we would start the routine over again. As evening approached, she would get something called Sundowner Syndrome. She would become irritable and confused and for a few hours each night she would want to fight and argue. That was quite a challenging time, I have to admit. She had a favorite little stuffed animal called a "pup ball" that she just loved. It was a soft, stuffed little brown puppy shaped like a ball with floppy ears and big brown eyes. During these difficult moments, I'd get out the pup ball, we'd bounce it around and 'boink' it on its head. Mom would laugh and laugh and those difficult moments would melt away. I remember, every morning when I greeted her, I would gently touch the side of her face and look into her eyes, telling her how much I loved her and her beautiful smile lit up the room. I used to sing to her the old song "You are my Sunshine" and she would clap her hands and smile and sometimes she would sing along with me. Those were very happy memories.

My mom suffered greatly with this disease and so did the rest of us, but she suffered with grace and through it all, she never lost her faith in God. Just writing this is so difficult, because I miss my mom so much; but I know she is in Heaven. The night she died, I went outside and looked up at the stars; they looked like hundreds of sparkling diamonds against a black velvet sky. As I stood there looking, they began to get bigger and brighter. It was as if someone had turned on a light switch. I smiled saying to myself "wow, someone just turned on all the lights in Heaven so Mom can find her way." I knew it wasn't going to be long now, so I went back into the house and sat down next to her bedside. I held her hand; I touched her hair and gently stroked her face. I kept telling her over and over "Mom, I love you. I love you so much." I knew that her hearing would be the last thing to go. So I just kept saying it over and over as I kissed her hands and her face. My dad and my daughter had fallen asleep. But, I sat there watching her every breath. One hour, two hours, three hours had passed. Then, I saw a change, I knew it was time. There were only minutes left. I needed to wake my dad quickly, so I woke him and my daughter and we all gathered closely around Mom as she took her last breath.

The few days after Mom's death were a blur. With all the family that came in for her funeral and the friends who gathered to celebrate her life, there was so much activity. I was worried about my dad but he held up very well. After all, my parents had been married for over 55 years. Even through the sorrow and tears, I kept saying to myself "death isn't the end, life goes on."

When my mother was born, her parents dedicated her to the Blessed Mother and they named her Mary Katherine. For the first seven years of her life she wore blue and white dresses in honor of Mary. My mother spent her life with a deep love and devotion to Mary. I always said that if I could be half the mother Mary was and the other half like my own mother, then I knew my own children would turn out great. My mom, like Mary, pondered in her heart many awesome, confusing and marvelous events in her life. She considered carefully what God wanted of her, and then she abandoned herself to Gods goodness in her life as wife, mother, daughter, sister, friend, aunt and so much more. She taught my sisters and I to also ponder, to consider and surrender, so that living our lives by her example, we might find the same blessedness that she found.

A couple of days after Mom's funeral, I was sitting outside and Mary, the mother of Christ, appeared, filling the sky. She was absolutely breathtaking. I had never been visited by Mary before and I was quite stunned at the details of her appearance. Her dress and veil were a blush pink color. I could see her face so clearly that I noticed her eyelashes, eyebrows, nose, lips, and her hair beneath her veil. Her hair was draped in front of her gown. I saw her facing sideways with her delicate hands folded as if she were praying. Mary stayed for the longest time. She didn't say anything, yet I felt such a beautiful, loving presence surrounding me and I was mesmerized by her beauty. I knew deep in my heart that she was letting me know that my mom was with her. Peace filled my heart.

What has comforted and sustained me throughout my grieving is to know where my mom resides after death. My faith is strong, and my near death experience tells me that life does go on. There are no words that can adequately describe the beauty and magnificence of my mom's home in Heaven. Nor can words describe what she's experiencing in that place. For now she is in the presence of God. How can I not be happy for her? Grief is a normal process and it comes in waves. It takes time; you never get over the loss of a loved one. It is a journey and it's a big one. Grief is an act of love, because we have loved deeply, we will also grieve deeply. Love never dies, because of her deep love for us; I know my mom is still with me, just in a slightly different way. Now I hold her in my heart instead of my arms. When I talk about my mom, I am honoring her. Even though she is not physically with me, she is never far from my mind and she is always in my heart. I remember the sparkle in her eyes, her beautiful smile, her words of wisdom and her warm, soft hugs that would make whatever was wrong, right again. My mom is the most beautiful part of me. I love her so much. God truly blessed me with the gift of such a wonderful mother.

CHAPTER 28

JOY COMES IN THE LITTLE THINGS
- MY HERO

Special Joys
By Sharon Milliman

As I sat in stillness, I watched a butterfly take flight.
It spread its wings of color and turned away the night.
And as it passed before me, I could clearly see just
how God changes difficult moments into special joys for me.

Since my near death experience, I have learned that Joy comes in the little things. I have also learned that it is important to share joy and happiness with others. These gifts are not meant to be held onto selfishly. Before you can share them with others, you must find them within yourself first. In other words, you cannot share something that you do not feel. For me, joy comes in the little things. Joy comes in the quiet moments, such as soaking in the first rays of the dawn, hearing the sweet song of a bird or listening to the gurgling of a stream as it flows over the rocks. These are the things that I notice when I spend a few moments alone with God. Such moments bring peace and harmony to my soul.

When I experience joy, happiness follows and it radiates out of me, like the rays of the sun that shines on others. Spreading joy only requires truly caring about someone else. It is found in a smile, a kind word, a good deed, by showing love and compassion. That is all it takes. Where there is love, one will find joy. That is where

I found my greatest joy. Someone else's joy became my joy. I found that real joy was in what I gave, not in what I received.

I was sitting outside drinking my coffee and enjoying the early morning sun when I noticed all the beauty around me. I noticed the soft breeze against my skin, the happy singing of the birds and the sweet fragrance of the flowers. It was a time of peace and quiet, a time to sit in the presence of God before I had to start my busy day. Later that morning I had left to run some errands. One of the places on my list was the doctor's office. While there waiting for some paperwork, I noticed a man standing in line waiting to sign in for his appointment. He had this look that I immediately recognized, although I wasn't sure why I immediately perceived overwhelming pain in his eyes and brokenness of his spirit. I felt this push to talk to him and heard a voice whisper, "tell him." So, I asked the man if he was a Vietnam Veteran. He said he was. I then asked him if he had a moment to speak about something important. He nodded and we stepped aside. I began to tell him that most of the military, fire and rescue servicemen today receive a hero's welcome, especially after the world trade center attack of 9/11. I wanted him to understand he was every bit as much of a Hero to me. I thanked him for fighting and for making so many sacrifices in the service to his country. I told him that I understood his pain, including his confusion about why certain things went so badly. I understood that he was just following orders by his commanding officer, that he was responding as any scared young man might, and that he was confused as to why he was sent to war. I ended by reiterating "You are my hero, thank you so much for what you did for all of us." At this point tears were streaming down both our faces. He hugged me and said, "Thank you. " He got back in line and I sat down.

When I was ready to leave a little while later, the man was also leaving his appointment. He walked up to me and said, "I wanted to thank you for all that you said to me. I had planned to end my life today, but you changed that for me. I am not going to do that now. I am going to stay now. So, thank you." He had such a new sparkle in his eyes and a smile on his face that gave me such incredible joy. We hugged each other again. As I was heading toward my car, I heard him whistling a song. Thank God! Whenever I think of him, and I do from time to time, I offer up a prayer of thanksgiving for him and all who have served in conflicts, wars or disasters. They are my heroes, all of them. Whether they were recognized or not, I am recognizing them now and saying "Thank you." Joy does come in the little things and it comes in acts of love towards others. That stranger gave me the most beautiful gift. He gave me joy. For his joy, became my joy.

CHAPTER 29

MIRACLES

Listen to the Wind
By Sharon Milliman

Listen to the wind as it whispers in the trees. If you quiet your heart, you will hear all the songs being sung in the softness of the breeze. For, it is in the silence that your soul will speak of the things that men often seek. The gift of your very presence marks your place as a person of worth. So, rejoice and be ever grateful for your journey here on earth. Spread your wings and lift yourself high, find your passion in the sky, and see the miracles in every living thing. Sing the song of your soul, for you know deep inside there is nothing to fear, allow your soul to fly free on the gentle wings of love. Open your heart, for you are a rising star shining bright for all to see. Fly like the eagle and you will be set free. Freedom is the way we all could be, if we let all things go. There are no strings to hold us bound. Quiet your heart and listen to the wind as it calls to your soul. For the message it gives is quite clear, "he who has ears, let him hear. When within the truth you live, it is love and joy that you give." Listen to the wind as it whispers in the trees. Sing the song of your soul, for all the songs of your heart will go out in the softness of the breeze.

I learned during my NDE that miracles happen every day. Every single breath I take is a miracle. I used to think of miracles in big magical terms like someone rising from the dead, or a mountain moving. The other problem was that I kept looking up for the miracle instead of looking inward and then, I would miss the miracle. God isn't up, He is right here with me, He is all around me. He is in everything I see and He is in me. Miracles don't have to be extra ordinary; if I open my eyes I will see miracles in the ordinary.

When, a sick child is healed by a young, impoverished mother's prayer; that is a miracle. When, a teenager says "no" to drugs and "yes" to higher education, that is a miracle. When I look at the divine spark in my own heart, I see another miracle. Indeed, miracles are everywhere and include everyone. As sons and daughters of God, we are all walking miracles. There is no need for me to look up to heaven for a miracle. I can see miracles in God glorious creation, from the delicate flowers that adorn the meadows to the majestic mountains that reach towards the heavens. I have touched the face of God when I brushed my fingers along the cheek of the woman I called "Mother" as she looked up at me with a lifetime of love mirrored in her eyes. I have walked hand in hand with God when I helped my mother walk when she could no longer walk by herself. These were beautiful miracles. I have looked into the eyes of God when I wiped away the tears from my daughter when she felt lost and afraid, another miracle. I have heard the voice of God in the wind as it whispers through the leaves on the trees and in the song of a bird in the early morning light. I can see the wonder of God when I see the dark, velvet night lit up with diamond stars and I see that they hold their place and never fall from the sky. That is a miracle. I have been touched by the love of God in the warm embrace of dear friends and family. I have felt the greatness of God in the highest mountains and in the deepest blue seas and in the birds that fly in circled flight, soaring to the sun with silvered wings, another beautiful miracle. During my NDE, when I said "God you made me, you are in me, so when I look in the mirror, I see you" that understanding was an amazing miracle. And when I have turned away from God in my loneliness, pain and sorrow, I find the miracle of miracles. Namely,

God has not abandoned me, for He is right there still holding me and I hear Him say "I will love you forever" and my heart is healed.

Sometimes miracles are extraordinary and inexplicable by today's science. After all, all things are possible with God. One big miracle in my life involved my sister. When my sister was a little girl she had an incurable kidney disease called Glomerulonephritis. My parents spent many sleepless nights and many long days in hospitals. As a young child, I remember we had to sit outside of the children's hospital in Chicago while the doctors did biopsies and treatments on her. I was quite sad that I was only allowed to wave at her through a window. Although, I understood that her immune system was compromised and having visitors could make her sicker, I missed my sister terribly. I remember feeling scared at seeing how frightened my parents had become. I remember crying buckets of tears while driving home from the hospital. Shortly thereafter, I remember kneeling down by my bed on a dark, quiet night, and I began praying. I asked God not to take my sister away. I told God I would give her my kidney and begged Him to please make her better. I believed with all my heart that He had heard my prayer and that He would answer my prayer and heal her.

My parents had also prayed for her every day. Although my sister was very young, she knew how sick she was. She was very brave, she never complained about the painful treatments and biopsies she endured. My sister used to sleep with her rosary wrapped in her hands every night. Her faith was very deep for one so young. I know that God hears every heartfelt prayer. At the age of 15 my sister was declared cured from the incurable kidney disease that nearly took her life. That was a miracle! God had answered our prayers. Today she remains healthy and happy. She is a wife, mother, grandmother and great grandmother. I now realize that my own sister, like the rest of us, is a walking miracle.

CHAPTER 30

Angels, who and what they are, and how they intervene

The Angel Within
By Sharon Milliman

The tenderest moments with Spirit will begin as soon as we come into the light of our own souls because this is where we will find our deepest passion, our most comfort, and the greatest love of our heart When we listen, the angels teach us about knowledge and ignorance and what separates us from them, they teach us about the dance of life and the stillness of being. They show us what is really in our hearts, our loves, and our hates, our freedom, and our smallness . . . the end of all journeys and the beginning of one true journey. They teach about walls we put up and what lies beyond them, about the known and the unknown. They teach about the believable and the unbelievable, about common sense and the uncommon senses, about what is pure and what is not, about what cries and what never will.

They teach us about forgiveness, how to forgive others and ourselves. And it is through their love and grace that we learn of the miracle of miracles. The angel within must be awakened to view the majesty of Paradise that exists beyond our senses, to hear the caring, nurturing voice of Truth that speaks flawlessly and continuously in the inner part of consciousness; and to feel the comforting breeze of peace blowing soothingly over the soul.

Our angel voices within come from a place where we do not think. They come from a "quietness" inside us and

all around us, from a place where love is cherished above
all else and come from a place of pure innocence and
perfection. This is the place where God lives in us. It is the
only place where the soul resides and the Truth is real.

God loves and knows me intimately. He speaks to me in specific
ways that I can understand. God speaks to me in the quiet moments.
He speaks to all of us in this way; we just have to open our eyes to see
it. Each one of us is very unique and special. Because we each have
special needs, God picks special angels with unique skills to protect,
help, communicate, and comfort us Angels have always been with
us since the beginning of time, in every time and in every culture.
There have been many people who have had angelic visitations while
others have been visited by their deceased loved ones, like Gray
Eagle. God sends us many types of helpers. With God all things
are possible.

Angels are created beings just as we are created beings. Their
essence is spirit and their station is angel. Angel simply means
messenger of God. One of the roles of my angels is to help me grow
and transform those parts of myself that needs healing. They see
things from a totally different perspective than I do. While I judge
something as being "good" or "bad," my angels discern events in
terms of golden opportunities for healing my anger, fear, and pain.
By highlighting the growth opportunities in my life, they help me
transform the negative into something positive.

Angels have numerous ways of communicating their messages
to us. For me, there have been times when I will hear music, even
when there is no music playing. Sometimes, I will smell the fresh
scent of flowers when there are no flowers around. At times, I will
hear an audible voice calling my name, when no one else is there but
me. Many times, I feel a presence or a gentle touch. These often feel
like a loving hug, just when I need it the most. Many times I will
get feathers, or heart shaped rocks, or even pennies from Heaven.

Over the years, I have found that angels are creatures of great action and very little words. Because their essence is spirit, they can take on human form and do whatever it takes to get the job done. But as soon as the job is complete, they vanish before one can say, "Thank you." They leave so that all the glory goes to God.

In 1970, at the age of eight, I became very sick with 106 degree fever. My dad was out of town and so my mom had taken me to the hospital. I remember the doctors and nurses rushing to put me on an ice mattress to reduce my fever. I spent two weeks in isolation until they could find the cause of the fever. I had inhaled a spore that lodged in my lung. It multiplied and caused a condition called Sarcoidosis. But during this time, my mom couldn't stay with me at night; I was alone in a strange, big hospital. I was so afraid. There was a young man who came every day like clockwork to take me to have my lungs X-rayed. He was very kind and made me laugh. After my X-ray, he would stay for a few minutes to visit with me. But late at night, I would wake up and find him sitting in the corner of my room. Amazingly, he was surrounded by a bright golden light. I was not afraid because I understood that he watched over me in tender love. He just sat there, quietly, until he vanished when I looked away. When I asked him about his night visits during the day, he would just smile. That's when I knew this man was an angel. One day, after having an X-ray, the angel put me back to bed, touched my hair, and told me that I would get better. Indeed, everything he said came true. Within a couple days the doctor said the spore count was shrinking and I was going home.

In 1982, when my oldest daughter was a baby, I had put her down for a nap and started fixing a pot roast for dinner. There was a splatter of grease that started a fire in the oven. The smoke rolled and filled our tiny apartment before I was able to put out the fire. The only thing I could think of doing was grabbing my baby and get out as fast as I could. I stood there on my porch holding my baby as the fire spread and black smoke billowed out of the front door. As I stood terrified, I noticed a tall man wearing a black trench coat and jeans. Oddly, he was walking with a very large timber wolf on a chain. Living in a very small neighborhood, I knew that I had never seen this man before. Nor would anyone in their right mind be walking a timber wolf on a chain.

The man walked over with his wolf and asked if he could help. I told him there was a fire in my kitchen, as I'm sure he already knew from all the smoke. He asked me to hold the dog leash. Looking into my ashen face, he said "it's ok, you'll be safe, she won't hurt you." I took the leash despite my fear. So, I'm standing there holding a baby on one side and a timber wolf on the other while this man walks inside my apartment. As fast as you can snap your fingers, he walks right back out again saying "Ok, the fire is out." I was stunned! He couldn't have even made it to the kitchen that fast. Then, he asked me "Do you want me to stay and help you clean up?"

I answered, "No I can get it myself, thank you." Nodding his head and smiling, the man took the leash. I thanked him for his help. He really didn't say much, he just smiled. I watched him walk his wolf down the street. I turned my head for just a second and when I turned back around, he was gone.

In 1990, I was driving down a country road early one morning taking my daughter to my sister's house before I went to work. I was driving down a very remote back road. It was a very cold morning in late January but the roads were clear of snow. As I was driving across a small icy bridge, my car went into a spin and then began to roll over and over across the road. As the car rolled, my seatbelt broke causing my face to hit the steering wheel and my head to smash through the windshield. I could feel the stinging, burning pain as the car continued to roll over and over. I could hear my daughter screaming, metal crunching and glass shattering in slow motion. I screamed out "Dear God, help us" just as the car slammed into the hillside by a creek. At the top of the hill was an old abandoned farmhouse. Unsafe, the house had long been condemned. Yet on this day there were many people milling about. As the people surrounded the car, a man lifted my daughter out of the back seat. She was unhurt. The man wrapped her in a blanket, gave her candy and tucked her warmly in his truck. Another person ran to call my work, my husband, and the ambulance. I found this very strange, as I had never given anyone these phone numbers. Since my seatbelt broke, I was half in the car and half out of the car by the time the car stopped rolling. A woman approached me, knelt down, held my head in her lap and wiped the blood from my face. I remember that her eyes were the color of the blue sky. I asked her if I was going to die. She told me that I would live. Then I asked her, "Has God forgiven my sins?"

The kind woman smiled and answered, "Yes, He has." The woman continued to gently hold my head as I went in and out of consciousness.

Finally, my sister arrived and retrieved my daughter. Soon, an ambulance arrived with a flurry of activity to get me to the hospital. I looked around for the kind lady so I could thank her. I asked my sister to find her but all the people who were by the farmhouse were now gone. There was no one there to thank! Although we left an ad in the newspaper to thank these good Samaritans, I highly suspect that they were not ordinary people. They were angels. I knew that angels don't stay around after the job is done. That's when I learned that angels are beings of great compassion and great selfless action. Here is another incredible point, as the woman wiped the blood from my face; she also healed all my facial wounds. With all of the injuries my head and face sustained that day, I have no scars.

When my mom was in the hospital after her first stroke, in April 2015, my dad and I sat by her bedside trying to decide the best options for her care. Dad was thinking about a nursing home for rehabilitative care but we weren't getting many answers from the attending doctors. Consequently, we were becoming more worried and frustrated. As mom seemed to be getting worse by the hour, the nursing home option seemed to be closing. As the hours passed, I kept getting the sensation of someone's hands pushing me out into the hallway. I kept hearing the word "hospice" very clearly, as if someone was whispering this word in my ear. This kept happening repeatedly until I finally walked out into the hall with no particular destination in mind. I soon met a woman all dressed in pink. She seemed to have a very bubbly personality. She greeted me with a huge, beautiful smile and sparkling eyes. She asked "Do you know what you need? You need a chocolate, mocha latte" she then led me into this little specialty shop hidden in a little corner of the hospital. She ordered the latte, handed it to me and asked me how I liked it. All the while, I couldn't help noticing how pink and round her pretty face appeared. She literally glowed in a pinkish hue. Then all of a sudden, the woman started talking about the importance of hospice for my mother. Specifically, she noted how my mom would be more comfortable at home in her own bed and she talked about how we as a family could best care for her. I asked the woman if she would speak with my dad about hospice. She replied "yes of course I will."

The woman and I went back to my mom's room to speak to dad. She began telling my dad all about hospice. When she finished, we thanked her for coming to talk with us and then she left the room. I immediately went out into the hall to thank the lady for the latte and the important information, but she had vanished. I even went to the nurses' station with the woman's name to find her, but they told me that no one by that name worked at that hospital. Moreover, no one had seen the woman I described. I believe that the lady in pink was an angel! There are a few reasons why I know this to be true. First, pink is my favorite color. Second, she couldn't have known about our need for hospice. Third, the drink was the best latte I had ever tasted. And finally, no one else had seen the woman despite her unique, beautiful glowing appearance. It is so awesome the way God sends angels, like the woman in pink, just when I need them the most.

One week after my mom died, my friend's grandmother was dying, so I went to the hospital to sit with my friend and her family. It was very hard to support my friend so soon after my Mom's death. But I needed to be there. Although I tried to be supportive, I began to crumble inside. The memories of watching my mom take her last breath came flooding back as did her burial. I told my friend that I needed to go. Thank God she understood. But no sooner did I leave the room than I began to have a full-fledged panic attack in the hallway. I couldn't breathe. It felt as if the walls began to move, the floor was coming up and the ceiling was coming down. I started to run, but the hall seemed to get longer and longer and I couldn't find my way to the elevator. I was crying so hard because I was no longer in the present moment. Rather, I had gone back to the moment my mom had died. I was reliving it all over again. All of a sudden a tall woman appeared. She was dressed, not surprisingly, all in pink. She asked, "How can I help you?" When I looked up at her, I could see a pinkish glow all around her and it made me stop sobbing. I told her "I can't find my way to the elevator." She said "come with me" and she helped me into the elevator. Then two more women, also dressed in pink, appeared. The first woman directed them to help me to my car. Then she disappeared. The other two women walked me outside and comforted me until I was able to finally control my emotions enough to drive home. As I got into my car, I turned to wave goodbye, but the two women had vanished.

There is another kind of angel that comes to my aide when needed. They are huge warrior angels that wear amour. In their manifestation, they resemble gladiators ready to do battle as God commands.

In 1999, I was being attacked by a very angry, young man. He had been taking drugs and his life was completely out of control. He lunged at me with a thick, wooden walking cane while screaming, "We are going to end this right here and now." All of a sudden I felt the warrior angels all around me. Then I saw two standing behind me and one across the room by the mantle. They were just enormous. As the young man took a step closer to strike me, he stopped dead in his tracks with eyes as large as saucers. That is when I knew he could see them too. A moment later he took that cane and broke it over his knee instead of hitting me with it. Pieces flew. One piece hit the mantle and bounced off the angel. While I called 911, the young man grabbed the two pieces of the wooden cane and ran out the door before the police arrived. Thank God for those huge warrior angels. If they had not come, I may not have been here today writing this book.

CHAPTER 31

FEAR

Become the mirror of truth and light
By Sharon Milliman

As I sit here in the night, another day goes floating by;
I look up and see the clouds rolling across the velvet sky
and twinkling stars peek out between cotton white; as
the winds of time blow night into day, day into night.

The night sounds play a sweetened tune,
as a hoot owl hoots and the opossums play.
Little bells ring in the night while
the wind chimes sing a sweet lullaby.

There is Peace in the air and all seems
well with the world tonight.

The wind blows softly through the trees
As a sweet fragrance wraps around me
from my head to my knees and as the gentle breezes
blow these words flow from the Heavens
"You are a mirror for others to see.
It is what they see that bounces off the
Reflection and comes right back to them from thee. So always
live your life in joy, and walk the path of truth and light.
Say to yourself, I am joy, love, truth, and
light, therefore, this is my life."

> If fear is the fire that you walk through, but
> you have faith and truly believe,
> you will not be burned, and in the raging
> waters you will not drown.
> For, He will lift you up on eagle's wings to a place
> where freedom reigns and peace exists.

I felt God's love so completely during my NDE that it filled every fiber of my being. When I returned to my body, I lived in such a profound Oneness with God that my bliss carried me for another several months. But when it was time to "come down off the mountain;" I had to learn how to integrate my experience with my everyday life. As spelled out in this book, that has proven to be very difficult at times over the years. I felt like I had one foot here and one foot still in the spirit world. It was hard to be in both realms instead of one or the other. There are many after-affects to having had an NDE, some will likely last the rest of my life. Before my experience, fear gripped my life almost to the point of paralysis. But since my near death experience, I no longer fear death. Physical death is a normal part of an eternal existence. It is nothing more than walking through another door in your house. When I died, I moved laterally and seamlessly. I didn't move up or down as a new being. My death happened so fast that I didn't have time to be afraid. Dying was so easy.

Since my NDE, I've learned that fear is just wasted energy. Now that I understand the bigger picture, I see things with spiritual eyes. I see human life with more loving compassion. I choose to live my life consistent with this larger reality by finding joy in even the littlest things. When fear encroaches on my day, I am now more cognoscente of where it is coming from and I stop the fear by readjusting my thoughts. I believe that fear does not come from God. Fear brings darkness to a sunny day. And where there is darkness, light cannot be. Even on the cloudiest days or during a raging storm the sun is still always shining above those dark clouds. In this manner, God's love is constant even when things in life seem terrible; His grace is unending and its forever. It is not in His will for us to be afraid. Fear and worry won't stop bad things from happening in life but it will stop me from enjoying the good things in my life. Removing all fear is easier said than done. But even in those moments where I do feel afraid, I find my comfort, my strength, and my courage through prayer. God always answers these prayers when I am open to Him.

In the quiet stillness of an early morning prayer I heard Gods voice as He said these words:

"My grace is sufficient. Do not be afraid. I love you and will never leave you. Be strong and hold steadfast in your faith for I created you and I am in you. I am in the ever present moment which is all eternity. No matter what is happening in the world with all its chaos, no matter what consequences may befall, I am in you and all around you. My grace and my love are constant, never ending. So be still and know that I am God and you are mine. Give me your burdens. I will carry them. I am strong enough to do so. And I will give you joy, for I love you with a love beyond your understanding. Don't be afraid. Fear does not come from me, it comes from a whole different place, so don't let it get in the way. Allow my grace to fill you and then peace will come."

If God's love is ever present and ever-lasting, then there is nothing to fear in the chaos of this world. All of the situations in our lives will come to pass. Only love transcends time; it is all that matters. In Gods voice, I was basically told to live boldly as a visitor of this world. Meaning, I am called to live in the world but not be of this world. If I have faith, I can give my burdens to God and He will carry them. And the things we fear come from a darkened world, not from the spiritual; fear does not originate from God. Only love comes from God. I know that if I keep my eyes focused on God and His radiant Light there is no time to focus on the darkness of fear. Focus on God's love and Light and you will find peace.

CHAPTER 32

No Greater Love

Everything I Want is You
By Sharon Milliman

I believe you made everything I can see,
all the mountains, valleys, and the deepest blue seas.
So, everything I want is you, alive in me....
Even when my eyes don't see,
I know you are there with me
that was your promise
and I hold it in my heart as true..
I believe with all my heart
It was for me that you were born;
It was for me you that you cried;
It was for me that your flesh was torn;
It was for me that you died.
You thought of me when you gave your last breath,
It was for me you conquered death;
It was for me you rose again and
I know that you will come again,
Just as you said you would do.
You loved me till death and I will praise your holy name.

So, everything I want is you, alive in me....
Even when my eyes don't see,
I know you are there with me
that was your promise

and I hold it in my heart as true..
I believe with all my heart
I know you are there with me, Jesus

As I was walking one afternoon, I saw a man approaching me. I recognized him right away, from all the visits we've had over the years and His breathtaking smile. It was Jesus, once again. He appeared at just the right moment. He began walking beside me and as He did we started talking. He knew my heart was breaking; it had been another long hard day of trying to cope with adjusting to living in this world after having been in Heaven. Life on earth seems so complicated sometimes. Jesus knows me so well; He always says the right things to lift me out of my dreariness. As we were talking, we came up to a side road and stopped to watch a scenario playing out involving a man and a young girl. Now, I don't know if Jesus created this scenario to happen to teach me some kind of lesson or whether it was actually happening. I can assure you it looked very real to me. As I was watching the scene before me, Jesus explained that the man was a pedophile and he had been eyeing the little girl with very evil intentions.

The little girl was on the same side of the street that we were standing on. She was playing with a ball between some cars parked along the curb. The man had been eyeing the little girl for some time and was about to make his move when he noticed a truck speeding down the road.

The little girl lost her ball out in the road so she went out into the road to get it. The man, seeing this, ran out into the road and grabbed the girl. He tossed her out of the way, just as the truck slammed into him, killing him instantly.

I asked Jesus if the man was going to heaven, Jesus said, "yes." I asked, "How is that possible, if that man spent his whole life as a pedophile, hurting little children?" Jesus, like a loving big brother, explained that the man, in his dying moment, made the choice to

126

save the little girl. By doing this one selfless act, he laid down his life for another. Jesus added, "There is no greater love than to lay your life down for another." Then Jesus said, "Oh and by the way, the little girl grows up to become a scientist who will find a cure for cancer. So, in that one instant, that man, who spent his entire life doing hateful, selfish acts, was able to change his soul, change his heart, and change his life. And in doing so, not only, did he change his own life, but, he also changed the course of history, changing many lives, many hearts, and many souls."

Jesus taught me that no human being, with our veiled and narrow perceptions, can ever truly know what is in the heart of another person. Only God knows the heart of a person, and only He knows how a person's heart can change in an instant. Only God knows all the secrets we hide in the chambers of our hearts. It only takes one act of love, one act of selflessness, to change the world.

How is it that Jesus knew the heart of this man, this pedophile? I believe Jesus is the Son of God. And I believe that knowing people's hearts is what Jesus does best. In my experiences with Jesus, He has challenged me toward good but has never condemned me for my sin or my faults. Rather, He sees me perfectly in my imperfection. That's how He sees all of us.

When Jesus walked the earth, He was a powerful presence. Many loved Him, many hated Him, and some even feared Him. But whatever the emotion, it was powerful. Jesus presents himself in many ways to many people. During my life, Jesus has presented Himself to me as a brother, friend, teacher, mentor, bridegroom, and lover of my soul. Jesus is someone who knows my inner most being. He knows me better than I know myself. He has been my constant companion throughout the journey of my life. He has always been by my side loving me and supporting me just as He had promised. He loves me and desires a personal relationship with me. Through my relationship, Jesus shows me that God is a personal being who loves me perfectly. Jesus teaches me that God is not only the Creator of all things, but He is my Heavenly Father who cares about me as an individual. Jesus shows us who God is. He brings us to the Father. That's what Jesus does.

Mighty is your power, gently is your way

Fear, death and darkness are what your death overcame. As you have said,

You are the Way, the Truth and the Life

All praise to you my Shepherd King and Holy is your name. It was for us all, that you came and forever we will praise your Holy name.

CHAPTER 33

Mists of Dawn

I Am...
By Sharon Milliman

I am not separate from my creation, any more than your thoughts
are separate from you.
I am not the reality behind the world but the reality that is in it.
For, I am in the world with you in all your life.
Wherever you are... wherever you go... wherever you look...
you can see me in the moon and in the stars that bring forth light
Out of the darkness,
you can feel me in the breeze that kisses your cheek.
And you can hear me in the flowing waters that heal, refresh and
renew.
The tiny seeds that grow into the mighty oaks contain my power
and the buds that blossom forth enfold my fragrance.
And you can feel me. I am with you every day of your life.
I am with you now... in the ever changing present that is true
eternity.
I am closer than the breath that brings your body to life, closer
than the thought that springs forth within the mind.
I am infinite. Closer than the beat that keeps your heart in tune.
For I am to be found- nowhere but, where you are.
I am the One that is all and can be seen in all, anywhere and
everywhere.
I am the all that is one I am in everyone.
For- I Am

Since my NDE God speaks to me in the beauty of His creation. Recently, my husband and I took a trip to see his dad in Virginia. I wrote down everything I saw while we were driving. Once again God lifted the veil and spoke to me through imagery. His message brought me hope and renewed my soul. He was telling me once again that He was with me during my life's peaks and valleys; I was never alone. As we drove, I saw the mist lying thick over the mountain tops and the tree branches were wet with the early morning dew. As the sun peeked through the curtain of white silk, the dewdrops glistened like diamonds, sparkling here and there. There was a stream flowing next to the road that gently curved its way through the trees and white foamy rapids played over the rocks. For miles it followed us, playing hide and seek as we went around the bends. A hawk, with its majestic wings outstretched, flew overhead, and down into another valley we went. There was a battle between the mist and the early morning sun. It had been a fair and good fight. The sun was stronger and had won the battle. Chasing away the mist, I could now see the endless crystal blue sky. As we continued on our journey, I noticed the huge rock formations on both sides of the road. I then noticed the life that sprang forth from within the rocks. I saw soft, bright green patches of grass interspersed among the brown, giving the earth the look of a patchwork quilt. A feeling of peace settled over my soul. I thought to myself "there is hope, always hope, even in the dead of winter, there is the hope of spring and new life". And so, the journey continued…

As we approached another valley, the mist returned thick and heavy, covering the trees and clouding my vision. The road was veiled by a thick, white blanket but my hope remained and my faith was strong, so I felt no fear. God was with me. I felt His presence near. Although we were under the thick, heavy mist the sky soon cleared enough for me to see that the sun was still shining, so beautiful and bright above the mist. The road ahead was clear and straight, nothing to hinder us, no danger to face. And I learned that it is through the dark valleys that we grow in faith. And it is by our faith that we find a measure of hope to keep us strong God's love is eternal and He never leaves us alone, He holds us up when troubles come, even in the mists of dawn.

CHAPTER 34

The Dark Night

Angel in the Dark Night
By Sharon Milliman

The sun has broken in your eyes
and will follow in your grace
Angels in the dark night will watch over you...
until the dark night delivers the day,
In tender arms they hold you tight.
Oh Child of my love,
I release you into Gods almighty hands.
To follow the path your precious heart demands.
And upon eagles wings you are lifted high.
Just remember who you are and hold your head up high
And speak your truth, my darling child, for
your beauty reaches so far and wide.
I am always near, and will always love you.
See this path before you with your heart and soul,
See it with love, and though the night is dark,
your true path will always be visible and bright.
The sun has broken in your eyes
and will follow in your grace.
Angels in the dark night will watch over you
until the dark night delivers the day,
and will follow in your grace.
Angels in the dark night will watch over you
until the dark night delivers the day.

In the dark night I cry out and I pray but sometimes I hear nothing and I feel so alone. Yet I know God is always with me, His love and grace are constant. I realize that I have been through moments like this before and the longing for Him is deep.

Some of the greatest mystics and holy people throughout the ages have endured the dark night of the soul. People, due to their limited human perspective, may view this as a terrible experience. But it is really a time for spiritual growth through self reflection and learning by trials.

The dark night is a time to experience a deep, deep longing for God and to learn to find meaning and joy in the longing. It's a time to remember past times of experiencing God's grace. The dark night is a time to trust the light of Christ within even though it's dark all around.

As I reflect on all I have experienced, I realize I'm no longer spiritually a child. I know that it's time for me to make some decisions about my life on my own. I do so knowing that God is right there with me. He doesn't have to tell me every single step to take. I must draw on the knowledge and wisdom I have gained over the years of walking my spiritual journey.

It is during these times that I remember all the things God has done in my life. I remember what He has taught me over the years. And I don't lose faith. I don't lose trust and I don't lose hope. I remember all the times He did speak to me. I remember when I sat with Him and the conversation we had during my near death experience. It is this remembrance that sustains me through this period of being in the desert. When I am in the desert, I pray that His Spirit will change my inclinations and strengthen me.

I realize that it is time for me to surrender to God's will during the dark nights. It is time for me to fully let go of all those things that hold me bound to all the things that no longer serve me. It is time to let go of those parts of me that cannot stand in the light of God and that separate me from Him. They are parts of me that only hurt my soul, such as anger, un-forgiveness, bitterness, selfishness, and regret. As I purge these negative emotions and feelings from my heart, I also realize that I must move forward beyond those painful parts of my life and release the memories as well. I must trust and accept that God, in His infinite love and goodness, will take care of all of it. As I breathe in His love, I exhale out all that needs to be released and I give it all over to Him.

And soon the dark night turns into a glorious new morning and I can, once again, hear that still quiet voice of God as the sun sparkles on the dew kissed grass. And God says, "I have always loved you. I have never stopped nor have I left your side, not for one moment. This day is my gift to you so be glad and rejoice in it."

Every day is a new beginning and every day we have the chance to say "yes." Being the fragile humans that we are we stumble, fall and fail. But, the fact that we say "yes" over and over as each new sun rises, allows us the opportunity to empty ourselves and become the vessel with which the Spirit of God can work in us and through us.

Saying "yes" to God takes a lot of faith. I have learned in my own spiritual journey that there are times when God not only gives graciously but He also takes away. He does this, not because He is a cruel and selfish God but rather, He is a loving, caring God who is helping me to empty myself of all the "things" in my life that keep me filled up.

If I am so full of "things," material possessions, relationships, regrets, hurtful memories and all of the business that life can bring then there is no room left for Him. It is my "yes" to God that begins this holy process of becoming an empty vessel. It is a painful process at times to empty oneself and certainly it isn't something that is done over night. It is a continual process of saying "yes" and trusting in God.

For me, the emptier I become the more I can become His hands, His feet, His eyes and sometimes even His voice to spread His message of love in this world.

After my near death experience, I had to lose everything only to find that what had been taken away was replaced a hundred times over by Gods precious love and His deep presence in my life. Again, I had said "yes" and I knew that He was with me every single moment of every single day. That had been His promise to me. I had faith. I believed He would do as He said He would do.

Eleven years have passed since my near death experience. There have been so many ups and downs, so many mountain moments and deserts. There have been many times when God stood right in front of me and I could see Him so clearly and other times when He was so far away that I felt like a hollow bone and my longing for Him was so deep. I would search and search but could not find Him no matter where I looked. But again, I said "yes" and I kept searching. During this period of searching for God, He was constantly reminding me of His love. He also reminded me of the conversation we had had while I was in Heaven so many years ago. Part of the conversation was as follows, "God, You made these people, You are in these people, so when I see these people, I see You." God smiled and said, "yes that's right." God was teaching me that He was not only in me but He was also in others. Because I had said "yes," God was teaching me to seek Him in the face and hearts of others and by doing acts of love for others, I am also serving God.

It is easy to say "yes "when you are on the mountain top. It is during these times I can feel God's presence and His love and it leaves me with a feeling of bliss and spiritual delight.

But, it is during the desert times, my dark nights of the soul, that I am aware that God has stripped away everything, even my being in Heaven with Him. When I returned to my body after my near death experience, it felt as though God had carried me for quite a while, but after several months, even that, He had taken away. I was completely humbled and laying flat on my face. And yet, even though I had absolutely nothing left and I felt so alone, I still said "yes." I loved God and even though I still searched and searched for Him, I believed with all my heart, He was still with me. He was there even though; I couldn't feel Him at all. There were no more words of love, no spiritual gifts, and no more mountain top moments, to carry me through. But I loved Him anyway. I knew in my heart, God would never leave. I clung to the memories and they helped me get through those times. The memories were of how good God had been in my life and in other's lives. And then I went about my life living my "yes" and trusting God.

Now, it is through others that I will find Him and in truth, God has never left me. I know this and hold on to this. One day another mountain top will come and more dark moments too. They say, it is in the valley that we grow. So, I will continue to walk my path in love with Him, living my "yes" and praising Him.

CHAPTER 35

FREEDOM OF FORGIVENESS

Angel of Grace
By Sharon Milliman

Angel of Grace, please guard us on our way
Show us the path of truth and light
Give us the strength to face our human plight.
Angel of Grace, your radiance is so bright
Allow us to hear your voice ever so pure and right
For your words are words of truth and might
Angel of Grace, come spread your golden wings
Spread your wings and lift us high
Lift us and hold us, help us to forgive
Release the pain, misery and strife
For forgiveness will set us free
Sweetest Angel, Angel of Grace.

It has now been eleven years since my near death experience and even though so much has happened over the years, in truth, I know that my journey has only just begun. I have learned a great deal during these past years but, there will always be more to learn. Forgiveness was one of those life lessons I really needed to learn. Through forgiveness there is the freedom of letting go. It allows healing for the body and the soul.

I learned that forgiveness is a creative act that takes me from being a prisoner of the past with hurtful memories to a strong, loving person, living in the present that is free of the chains that kept me bound, and is now at peace. It doesn't mean that I condone the hurtfulness. It means that I have moved beyond it. Forgiveness is one of the most significant, healing processes that I have gone through in my life. There have been times when the hurt was so deep that I knew I couldn't do it by myself. Forgiveness is a process. The 'will' to forgive is the first step and in some instances, it has taken a lot of prayer and a lot of help from God to be able to take that step. I know that being able to forgive will bring peace to my soul and harmony to my life. There have been times in my life where I needed to forgive others, even when they didn't ask for forgiveness. That can be challenging, but even more challenging is forgiving myself.

Un-forgiveness feels like a heavy chain that keeps me held bound. It keeps me trapped in a place and time that only hurts me. It is a chain which causes negative feelings to grow and fester inside my heart. Holding on to past hurts can cause anger, bitterness, feelings of betrayal and a sense of abandonment or separation from the love of God. That isn't what I want in my life, nor is that what God desires for me.

Forgiveness is not a requirement, but it *is* something that I feel I need for my own soul's growth. When I am able to forgive, God's healing flows through me, and around me; and I become aware that I am now free from the chain of un-forgiveness, that has held me bound for so long. When I forgive, I am free to send unconditional love out into the world around me and I am now able to experience the natural flow of God's divine love dissolve all the hurt, all the bitterness, all the pain and the sense of being wronged. Even though Gods grace is constant, because of my un-forgiving heart, I felt a sense of separation, but now, I am able to once again feel His grace pouring onto me and flowing through me, forgiving through me. Because I have opened my heart and have forgiven, there is no more of this illusion of separation. There are no more feelings of abandonment. God's love healed all of it.

For me, forgiveness is the greatest form of unconditional love and acceptance and it is the key to true happiness. Forgiveness is the chance to begin again, to create a new and bright future, and a beautiful new life.

CLOSING REMARK

My near death experience has demonstrated that there are many ways to connect with God through love. But I would be amiss not to emphasize the power that Jesus had during my daily walk. As I conclude my book, I wanted the reader to understand that Jesus is not just some historical figure that lived two thousand years ago. My relationship was so intimate that I needed to share it with others. In doing this, I hope that others may also find a personal relationship with Jesus. Not only do I hope that others find a personal relationship with Jesus, but with all the loving hosts of Heaven. For me that includes God, Jesus, angels, and deceased loved ones. We all have a loving host backing us, rooting for us and helping us through this tough schoolyard called earth.

My prayer for you is that through the writings and messages in this book, that you will discover the loving messages that are meant for you. I pray that you will receive hope and a feeling of renewal deep in your soul knowing that God loves you as if you were the only one He ever created. May you always know what a cherished blessing you are to God and to all whose lives you touch.

May God keep you safe in the palm of his hand, may the warm winds of the Heavens flow around you and the sun rise up to greet you. May the little birds sing their songs of Joy, and may your days be filled with Love, Peace, and Beauty all the days of your life.

1 https://en.wikipedia.org/wiki/Kenahkihin%C3%A9n
2 'Prayer Changes Us and we change things'
Mother Teresa's wisdom and New Thought by Diane Bishop
http://www.harvbishop.com/?p=25

ABOUT THE AUTHOR

Sharon Milliman was born in Ohio as the middle daughter of three girls. Currently married, Mrs. Milliman has two adult daughters and lives in West Virginia. Mrs. Milliman worked in the banking industry for over fifteen years. After she retired from her job, Mrs. Milliman became involved with the foster-care program and has volunteered for many years at area hospitals and churches, giving back to her community. She had also spent several years as a home health caregiver, caring for her aged parents, specifically her mother, who had end-stage Alzheimer's. For two years, Mrs. Milliman served on the board of directors for a nonprofit organization called the Wings of the Whispering Wind, an organization dedicated to creating a model for an eco-friendly, self-sustainable community.

Because she has had two near-death experiences, she has been a guest on several radio shows as well as working closely with Joseph Varley at Klay AM Talk Radio on a show called Joseph Varley Presents, where they have presented several shows about near-death experiences, life and death, and life beyond death. Most prominently, Mrs. Milliman was featured on the National Geographic Channel in a show titled Return from the Dead about near-death experience. The show aired in the April 17, 2016. Mrs. Milliman has presented as a guest speaker at a number of spiritually oriented groups, including the IANDS group in Raleigh, North Carolina.

Because of having two near-death experiences and numerous spiritually transformative experiences, Mrs. Milliman has a deep interest in how God moves through the lives of herself and others, making her a pilgrim and supporter to many within the NDE community as well as her broader community. She does this through listening, giving voice to her experiences, and through her inspirational writing. Mrs. Milliman plans to continue her work to promote God's unconditional love to a hurting world.

Printed in the United States
By Bookmasters